Ragged Road

Ragged Road

A Journey Toward Faith & Love

DENNIS LEAVER

Edited by Robert J. Leaver

RESOURCE *Publications* • Eugene, Oregon

RAGGED ROAD
A Journey Toward Faith & Love

Copyright © 2025 Dennis Leaver. All rights reserved. Except for brief quotations in critical publications or reviews, no part of this book may be reproduced in any manner without prior written permission from the publisher. Write: Permissions, Wipf and Stock Publishers, 199 W. 8th Ave., Suite 3, Eugene, OR 97401.

Resource Publications
An Imprint of Wipf and Stock Publishers
199 W. 8th Ave., Suite 3
Eugene, OR 97401

www.wipfandstock.com

PAPERBACK ISBN: 979-8-3852-3314-4
HARDCOVER ISBN: 979-8-3852-3315-1
EBOOK ISBN: 979-8-3852-3316-8
VERSION NUMBER 01/02/25

Scripture quotations are from The ESV® Bible (The Holy Bible, English Standard Version®), © 2001 by Crossway, a publishing ministry of Good News Publishers. Used by permission. All rights reserved.

Special Permission granted by Tau Publishing; Carmel, Indiana for use of previously published material from *Hidden Beauty*, by Fr. Rick Martignetti, OFM, 2013.

To those who continue to run the race against cancer.
Let us not grow tired in running our own race,
but instead encourage those around us.

Contents

Preface | ix

1. Wilderness | 1
2. Harvard Medical School—Sort of | 15
3. Secrets Unraveled | 28
4. Forgive Us Our Debts | 33
5. AC/DC | 38
6. Into the Green Unknown | 46
7. Seeds of Change | 56
8. Unseen Grace | 61
9. A New Dawn | 67
10. Solar Eclipse | 74
11. Ruins to Renewal | 80
12. Jerusalem | 86
13. Skating on Thick Ice | 98
14. Meeting Ernie | 105
15. The Ripple Effect | 114
16. Multiplying the Loaves | 123
17. Medical Supplies and Miracles | 131
18. Wilderness to Grace | 140

Bibliography | 143

Preface

LIFE IS OFTEN DESCRIBED as a journey, one filled with unexpected twists and incredible discoveries. As I reflect on my own journey, the path of faith and love has led me to places I never imagined. It is this journey that I wish to share with you through "*Ragged Road: A Journey Toward Faith and Love.*"

The idea for this book was created out of a deep desire to document and share with you the transformative power of faith in my life. Over the years, I have encountered numerous obstacles that tested me and sometimes pushed me into the darkness. Yet, it was through these very trials and difficulties that I discovered the endless depth of God's love. My hope is that by sharing my story, I will encourage you to explore the exciting potential for growth and redemption in your own life.

This book is a collection of stories of my personal experiences woven together from my early years growing up in Rhode Island, through my career in radiation therapy, to the profound moments of betrayal and forgiveness. The Allagash Wilderness Waterway, Yosemite National Park, and the streets of Providence are more than just settings; they are almost characters in themselves, adding depth and texture to the narrative. These places hold a special significance in my life, as each played a part in my painful prodigal son experience, spiritual growth and understanding of love.

Writing this book helped me focus on the call to serve–to learn–and to create. My call is to serve God. You may have a

Preface

different calling. This book aims to help you discover a calling–whatever it is. The stories are true-life experiences; some I hope you will relate to from your own past encounters, prompting you to dare explore deeper. This process of storytelling was not undertaken alone. I owe a huge debt of gratitude to my family, friends, and mentors who provided solid support and encouragement. Their belief in me kept me grounded and motivated. I had to discard some of the masks I concocted over the years to uncover the real truth. At times it was a bit frightening and scary.

To you, the reader, I extend my deepest thanks for embarking on this heartfelt journey with me. I hope that as you turn each page, you find reflections of your own trials and triumphs. May this book serve as a reminder that no matter how ragged the road, faith and love have the power to heal us and transform our lives. You might be invited as you read, to consider the ways in which faith has shaped your own path, and the moments where love has powerfully penetrated your being. Together, let us explore these transformative forces and unravel the beauty that lies within the journey.

Thank you for joining me on this path. May you find hope, healing, and strength within these pages.

1

Wilderness

1984

THERE WERE EIGHT OF us on my first trip to the Allagash, a journey George organized annually each spring, as the Allagash Wilderness Waterway awoke from its winter dormancy. In the spring, several types of mayflies became prevalent in streams and rivers, signaling the beginning of prime wild trout fishing season. Trout love mayflies, and George loved trout.

George was a man of many passions and delightful quirks. He was aging slowly, showing signs of an unhealthy lifestyle—a small limp from a bum knee and a noticeable pot belly. He was nearly bald, with an uneven amount of wispy hair scattered over the sides of his head. He was mostly quiet and reserved. A lifelong lover of the outdoors, he spent countless hours relishing the challenges of fly-fishing. His stories were usually full of more detail than needed but were often entertaining. His barbershop, located three blocks from L.L. Bean was a hub of community life, where banter and tall tales flowed freely. In one corner of the shop, complete with barber's pole out front, he had dedicated a small space to tying flies used to catch the right fish with the right fly—an art and a science, according to George.

He had a knack for securing the best equipment. Each year, he borrowed as many canoes and as much camping gear as needed from Bean's flagship store in Freeport. Thanks to his mother's long-standing employment, he easily secured slightly used Old Town fiberglass canoes that were rugged, dependable, and perfect for our adventure. She lived alone, after George's father died, two blocks from her only son and his two children. Bean's encouraged its employees and family to evaluate the equipment in the rugged outdoors.

The drive to Telos Lake, our starting point, was an adventure in itself. We stayed overnight in a church hall in the small town of Eagle Lake before embarking on our three-hour journey over gravel roads that meandered through the Northern Maine Woods. The logging roads controlled by paper companies, were rough and unforgiving, with "travel at your own risk" signs and the constant threat of flat tires and no gas stations.

We stopped at a toll gate at the beginning of our grueling gravel road trip and paid a fee to the paper company for using the road, in addition to the fee for shuttling our van from Telos Lake to the village of Allagash, where we hoped to arrive eight days later. This was my first trip, and I was a bit nervous about traveling in the wilderness since we were nearly seventy-five miles away from civilization and likely more than one-hundred-fifty miles from any hospital. My mind wrestled with the uncertainty.

The van ride over the wide, gravel roads, crammed with gear and people, was dusty and uncomfortable. My seat, just a bucket turned upside down between the two front seats, left me jostling with every bump and turn. I was probably assigned the seat because I was the smallest, weighing in at around one-hundred-forty-five pounds. By the time we reached the lake, my butt hurt. My nerves were as frayed as the roads we'd traveled. It was good to stretch and get our gear ready.

As we ventured deeper into the Allagash Wilderness, two to a canoe, the signs of human habitation quickly faded away, leaving us traveling with the fast-paced current downriver in near-complete natural isolation. The beauty was stunning.

Wilderness

As I paddled through the dark waters, the scene around me revealed a supernatural aspect of nature. We all enjoyed visiting a place that was less touched—something was inviting me into this vast wilderness. The rhythm of my paddle slicing through the water created ripples that quickly faded behind the canoe. The shore was a tapestry of lush greenery, a mix of evergreens and hardwoods. Along the water's edge, the underbrush was thick with ferns, wild blueberry bushes, and various native plants. Patches of sunlight filtered through the canopy of leaves, casting shadows on the forest floor. The shoreline was punctuated by rocky outcrops and sandy coves, where the water lapped against the rocks and sand.

In some spots, fallen trees extended into the water, their gnarled branches providing natural perches for birds and other wildlife. George had warned us to stay clear of these dangerous river traps. The distant call of a loon echoed across the water; its unique cry added to the sense of remote serenity. Overhead, an eagle or osprey soared gracefully, scanning the water for fish. The sky above was a brilliant blue, with a few white clouds drifting by.

I felt a deep connection to God and the natural world, surrounded by the timeless beauty of the Maine wilderness. The sense of peace and solitude was overpowering, making the beginning of this trip feel like a gift from God.

Each heavy-laden canoe was loaded with food and gear for our eight-day adventure. George recommended storing sleeping bags in sealed five-gallon mud buckets, typically used to hold sheetrock plaster. I heeded his advice, not wanting to sleep in a wet, soggy sleeping bag.

Everything I needed was carefully packed to fit snugly around me in the canoe while balancing our load on the river. The vast stretches of dense forests, massive lakes, and wildlife created an ethereal, peaceful experience of pure and untainted beauty. At one point, my steadfast partner Tom and I fell behind the group as we enjoyed the scenery and relaxed into the packed gear positioned behind us, drifting comfortably down river with our feet up, basking in the sun, only to be warned by the approaching warden to keep our group in sight. Up to this point, we had not seen any other canoeists.

Tom embodied a serene yet commanding presence. Standing just over six feet and weighing two-hundred pounds, he had the look of someone who watched what he ate and exercised regularly. He resembled a lumberjack with his strong brow and muscular arms. His parents, both from a sturdy French background, were descendants of earlier settlers who had migrated from Canada in the mid-1800s. His quiet demeanor and rugged features reflected a deep, somewhat-shy personality that harmonized with the natural world around him. He loved the outdoors. Tom's extensive knowledge of kayaking, coupled with his passion for fishing and hiking, made him an invaluable companion on the river. On this trip, he confidently guided us from the stern position, navigating through the waterways with a skillful hand. He didn't talk much as we glided together along the river.

The Allagash River runs ninety-two miles long and, interestingly, it is one of a few rivers in the world that flows in a northerly direction. It then empties into the fast-paced St. John River, about a dozen miles from the Canadian border. This river creates the somewhat jagged boundary line seen on every map, marking the northernmost edge of the United States. Today, the river remains largely untouched by human development. It has preserved its natural beauty, with pristine landscapes of huge forests of spruce, fir, and pine stretching as far as the eye can see, interspersed with crystal-clear, mile-long lakes.

Wildlife thrived here—moose, black bears, wild brook trout, and bald eagles roamed freely. While I longed to see moose, the thought of encountering a protective black bear sent shivers down my spine. On the third day, we navigated two large lakes before reaching our campsite upriver from Churchill Dam. I spotted my first moose near the outlet of Eagle Lake—a mother and her calf wading close to shore. I lingered, patiently capturing the moment with my 35-mm camera.

George had arranged for one of the park rangers to transport our gear nine miles downstream the next day, allowing us to tackle

Chase Rapids with empty canoes. The rapids were a mix of class I and II whitewater, with rocks and chutes that tested our skills. Our fiberglass canoes, known for their maneuverability, bumped over rocks with ease, but George's warnings about the dangers of "broaching" kept us alert. This is where the force of the water could easily capsize or pin the canoe sideways against a rock.

The river resembled a rock garden with large boulders protruding out of the water. We found that the key to staying dry was navigating the relatively narrow s-shaped path downriver and then turning quickly when an obstacle was in sight. To do this, I had to communicate to Tom in the stern quickly and effectively. It was exhilarating to run the rapids together, which took longer than we expected. Tom and I did take on some water, but not enough to capsize the canoe during the nearly two hours needed to shoot the rapids and emerge at the mouth of Umsaskis Lake. Three of the four canoes made it through the rapids dry. The one that went for an unplanned swim regrouped and caught up to our gear stacked near a flat part of the river. The two companions emerged soaking wet but unharmed. They were grateful their gear was on the riverbank and not with them in the canoe. Challenging Chase Rapids taught us to read the whitewater and pay attention to our surroundings.

Along the trip, we explored several sites depicting early logging activity in northern Maine. We stopped at the Tramway, a historic timber-transport system built in the early 1900s. It was designed to move large timber between Eagle Lake and Chamberlain Lake. The challenge of moving large trees to market changed once lumberjacks began using Maine's rivers and waterways more effectively. Prior to this, ropes, horses or oxen were used to move the timber. Some lubricated the logging road or forest floor with water or grease to help transfer the heavy logs. Pine and oak could be used for shipbuilding (especially the mast), cedar used for shingles, and spruce and fir could be turned into pulp for making paper. Everyone used paper!

Most campsites, located along the river's edge, were primitive and provided a pleasing view of the river. The sound of the running water usually helped us get a good night's sleep. Because we began each morning just after sunrise to avoid the wind on the lakes, we had plenty of time later in the day, after setting up our tents, for fishing and swimming—especially near the unspoiled natural setting of Allagash Falls. Reaching the falls was one of the highlights of the trip.

At mile seventy-eight along the river, we stopped at the designated takeout point about a thousand yards before the falls for a time-consuming, challenging portage. This was our only substantial hike along the river bank, carrying our canoe. It was not your traditional waterfall, but instead dropped gradually over a span of about two-thousand feet. I found out later that there were two fatalities earlier that year when a father and son failed to navigate their portage around the falls.

For the lengthy portage, George came prepared with a small two-wheel contraption that effortlessly guided the packed canoes filled with all our gear. He could no longer make the portage the traditional way—hand carrying the canoe and gear separately because of his back. We spent a fair amount of time that day at the falls moving our stuff, eating lunch, and fishing. It was surprisingly warm, sunny, and mesmerizing. The high spring water that year pounded the rocks repeatedly, creating a cool misty river fog and an unending mighty roar as the river cascaded across several large drops of eight to ten feet.

Fishing at the falls was a challenge for me, as I did not know how to fly fish like some of the others. Both George and Tom had success fly-fishing in the small pools beyond the falls. They made it look so easy, moving the fly attached to the special line back and forth over their head. The fish were not interested in good old-fashioned worms that day. So, I just put my pole down, propped it up against a small tree located near our launch point scheduled later in the day, and decided to rest instead.

I enjoyed the unusual warmth of the sun in late May, quietly re-reading Psalm 139, which I had prayerfully pondered earlier that morning. I was trying to practice being still and quieting my spirit as I relaxed on one of the large flat rocks near the last substantial drops in the falls. Even the rocks were surprisingly warm. Growing up, I had always found it difficult to be still in whatever I was doing. I think it was my hyperactive brain waves that kept me moving from one thought to another. The thoughts were constantly darting from one lobe of my brain to another.

Being still, I learned, goes beyond the physical act of remaining motionless. This was what I was trying to do on the rock. It was about quieting my mind and allowing myself to become attuned to the deeper rhythms of the unspoiled beauty around me. I was anticipating that if I had a long moment of spiritual stillness, the incessant chatter in my brain would fade away and be replaced by a profound sense of peace and contentment. The more I practiced this type of contemplation, I found that I could sometimes create a type of sacred space where one can listen to the whispers of the heart. The warmth and bright sunlight made me drowsy and quieted my spirit. Although the words of the Psalm resonated with my innermost being, "O Lord, you have searched me and know me! You know when I sit and when I rise up; you discern my thoughts from afar. You search out my path and my lying down and are acquainted with all my ways." (Ps 139:1–3). God was nudging me and speaking to me as I lay on the warm rocks, preparing me for a tremendous challenge that was yet to come later that day.

George, having caught several fish on a new fly, gave us the ten-minute warning, as he usually did, before we prepared to depart for our next campsite, McKeen Brook, a short two-thirds of a mile downriver. About half of us in the group caught fish, which we would all snack on before dinner. The fresh trout fried in a pan with a little butter smelled so wonderful. All the campsites on the river were first-come, first-served. There was no reservation system. If the site was not available, you moved on to the next site. I was learning from George, our veteran guide, that we put our canoes in the water early each day for a reason—just after sunrise—so we could choose the best campsite and avoid the strong winds late in the day.

It unfolded as George had planned—our preferred site was available. After setting up our tents and organizing our gear, I realized I had left my fishing pole, borrowed from my brother Don, at the falls. Tom was still fussing with his tent and the abundance of black flies swarming everywhere around him when I explained my problem. I told him it would not take me too long to hike back upriver to the falls, grab the missing fishing pole, and return. He nodded toward me, acknowledging that he heard me. After all, it was only a little more than half mile upriver, and I had acquired some basic skills as a Boy Scout and had used them on many camping trips. My plan was to keep the river in sight on my right as I made what I thought would be a one-hour hike to the falls and back. I would soon learn that in the wilderness, everything was different.

Little did I know how difficult a hike it would be. It started out fine—following a narrow path illuminated by bright sunlight along the river's edge. The water was running swiftly, as it does in the spring, creating a pleasant rumbling noise. The unmistakable sound was both invigorating and soothing, evoking a sense of nature's raw power and beauty. Within a short time, I lost track of the river since I had to traverse over and around large downed trees. It made moving more slowly through the uncharted wilderness forest much more difficult. There was no longer a narrow path, just dense vegetation, thick undergrowth, and towering trees that filtered a small amount of sunlight, creating a beautiful pattern on the forest floor. Fallen trees, tangled roots, and rocky outcrops made it a challenge to hike quickly. Crossing small streams created even more difficulties. Black flies were everywhere, nudging me to secure my bandana across my nose and mouth in an attempt to breathe better without inhaling the little buggers. I had applied high-quality bug spray just before I departed, but all kinds of insects, some I had not encountered before, found me anyway. At times it was hard to see with so many bugs buzzing around my head and darting into my face.

I had never seen foliage so thick and dense. Was this short hike going to get worse? More times than not, I walked above the forest floor along the moss-covered downed trees, still sturdy enough to hold my weight. It became too difficult to walk on the ground and choose to either duck under or climb over large downed trees. It turned out to be so dense that I decided to walk along one tree to the next, zig-zagging my way along to the falls. It was like walking on a balance beam—then another and another at various heights and odd angles. To me, it seemed quicker. Sunlight was no longer filtering through the trees, and a type of low-level river fog was settling in, making it even more difficult to keep the river in sight. Although I could still hear it, I grew increasingly nervous as the hike turned into an unexpected ordeal.

My lightweight daypack contained water and some trail mix allowing me to refuel during my short rest at a small clearing. Without a watch, I estimated I had been hiking for about forty-five minutes. I should have reached the falls by now. At this point in my journey, the river fog made it nearly impossible to use the sun as a directional aid and I could no longer see or hear the river. My focus shifted to other sounds like rustling leaves and snapping twigs. I was growing nervous and concerned. My heart raced more, beating noticeably quicker and louder, and my dark thoughts wandered.

I tried to recall exactly what George had said to do if we encountered a bear. Although it was difficult to think straight, I did remember him saying we should remain calm and not run. Make yourself look bigger by standing up tall, raise your arms in the hope of intimidating the bear. Lastly, keep facing the bear as you slowly back away, not turning your back. Whatever you do—don't run.

More negative thoughts drifted back and forth, as fear clouded my mind much like the river fog that surrounded me. I had relied on my pride and Boy Scout skills that were not working. The atmosphere felt gloomy. Insects continued to buzz around me, and the occasional rustle of leaves hinted that something unseen was moving through the underbrush not far from me. My pulse and respiration had increased even after taking a break and resting. Fear was now in control, as I began to think about what might be moving through the underbrush.

Was I being stalked by one of Maine's carnivores, like a black bear or maybe a Canadian lynx? In this era before cell phones, I began to imagine that I would be attacked, painfully ripped apart, and would never be found. I was convinced I would not stand a chance if I crossed paths with a bear or lynx. No one would ever find what remained of me. These thoughts consumed me and fed the fear.

As I imagined my death approaching, I truly felt like I was the first person to have ever walked in this part of the Allagash Wilderness. The fallen trees and terrain were unlike anything I had ever witnessed before. The air was filled with the earthy scents of soil, the fragrance of pine, damp moss, and decaying leaves. My confidence was also decaying rapidly. I constantly imagined that I was walking where no man had ever walked before. How did I get here?

There was a battle going on in my mind. My thoughts were dreadful and discouraging. I was hearing things like, "You're no good," "You're lost," "No one is going to find you." All I could do at this point was to move where I thought was forward toward the falls. Without the sun or sound of the river, which way was I to go? I wanted to continue to trust that God would make a way where there seemed to be no way. This was my racing heart's prayer. I knelt down on the moss-covered ground and prayed for help, a sign, a miracle from an unseen God—admitting that I was totally lost.

I remained still for a moment to look and listen, but I didn't see or hear the river—nothing. More gloom invaded my thoughts. Just as I began to move again, I heard the rustle of leaves directly in front of me. A good-sized dark brown animal elevated itself off the ground, making a loud sound as it moved up the front part of my body, touching my legs and chest, and then landed several feet in front of me. Intense panic gripped me as I fell backward. It was difficult to breathe, and I could feel my heart pounding loudly. What was that? Although my sense of awareness was very keen, I was frightened and feared for my life. The fight-or-flight adrenaline had kicked in, coursing through my veins—increasing my heart rate and respirations even more. All my heightened senses were in overdrive.

Laying on the ground on my side, I could see before me what looked like a large dark reddish-brown colored type chicken, and I could sense a slight wetness between my legs. When that bird fluttered up—triggering every nerve ending in my body—I imagined I was being attacked by a bear and would surely die.

I would later learn it was a partridge. It had a large round body—almost pregnant-looking—very short legs, and a small head containing sharp eyes that were now scanning me for danger. The partridge was on what looked like a narrow path a few yards in front of me and remained very still. I could see more of a path just beyond this strange-looking animal. I had never seen a partridge before; I had only heard of the one we sing about at Christmas.

This was utterly amazing—where did this path come from? It hadn't been there a moment ago, only dense brush and downed trees. At this point, I too remained very still and cautious, trying to recover from my near-death experience. Neither of us moved for some time, but just stared at each other. This was so unexpected. Part of me was glad it was just a bird that likes seeds, insects, and other small food items.

Amazingly, I heard a small still voice speaking in my heart, saying, "Follow this bird—it will lead you." It was like no other encounter I had experienced in the woods before. I had new faith in the voice and the bird. My fear diminished as I thought of following the bird. I was hopeful.

As I stepped slowly forward on the path toward my new friend, she fluttered a bit and flew about ten yards further down the path. I followed obediently. This same pattern went on for some time; the bird leading and me following until I could hear the faint sound of the river's flow to my right. When I looked up again to thank my friend, she was gone. To my amazement, I could now see the river clearly through the trees. What a pleasing sight and welcoming sound. Not long after, I could hear the louder water of Allagash Falls. When I reached the falls, I found my fishing pole just where I had left it, leaning against a small tree. Now, how to get back to camp?

Walking the half-mile back up toward the beginning of the falls would allow me to see if other groups were in the midst of their portage. If so, perhaps I could hitchhike downstream to rejoin my group at McKeen Brook. Unfortunately, there were no other people running the river this late in the day. One group of campers near the falls indicated they had not seen anyone pass through the portage area in the last hour or so. Perhaps I could float downriver on a log to the campsite. There was no way I would hike back! When I returned to the spot of my now-found fishing pole, I spotted what I thought might be a canoe coming upstream through the fog. I became excited.

George in the stern and Tom in the bow appeared eerily out of the river mist. They had made the half-mile trip upstream against the river's current to find me. I was ecstatic. Wow, was I grateful to see them. We exchanged hugs and quickly started back in the gray dim light remaining. It was very quiet on the river as dusk set in. The way back to camp, traveling with the current, was smooth and effortless. George gave me an earful, telling me how worried he became. I humbly listened, as he reminded me how foolish I was. He sternly said, "People get lost in these woods all the time, Dennis. I can't believe you did this. Are you that stupid? Just last year, three teenagers were exploring and hiking not too far from here and were never found. They searched for days." I apologized to our guide over and over all the way back to camp; I felt foolish.

Around the fire that evening, I shared my grueling experience with the group and took my medicine for acting foolishly—trying to hike to the falls on my own. The humility was uncomfortable but healing. They got a kick out of my encounter with the partridge. But it was Tom, who I had confided in on the trip back from the falls, who surprised us all by sharing his heart around the fire that night. "Our help comes from the Lord (Ps 121:2)," he proclaimed loudly in a steady confident voice. He stood up, had everyone's attention, took a very deep breath, remained still for some time, and continued, "even though Dennis was trying to solve his problem on his own, God was right there with him, guiding him. Oftentimes, we don't always see that far out in front of our situation or around the next bend or along the twisting path in life. We often can't see beyond a few weeks or months, but God can."

"If we trust God, he will always show us the way. All we need to do is ask," he asserted, his voice filled with conviction. "Now, I too pray for guidance daily and seek advice from friends and family instead of trying to solve my problems on my own." He paused, his eyes moistening, reflecting a deep, hard-won battle. "Some of you know, several months ago, well actually, one-hundred-twenty-five days ago today, I was struggling with a drinking problem. I thought I could handle it by myself, but I kept slipping back and falling. It wasn't until I surrendered and sought help that I began to find my way back. God led me to the support and strength I needed through the twelve-step program. It saved me"

His story resonated deeply within me. I realized that God directs our path and guides our feet. Wandering in the woods provided a powerful lesson—we are not alone in our struggles, and by seeking God's guidance and the support of those around us, we can overcome even the greatest of challenges.

Taking out his harmonica, we listened while Tom poured out his heart in a riff that had come to me in prayer—one that I had jotted down and shared with him earlier in the trip. After he played the song, there was complete, utter silence. All you heard was the crackling of the fire for some time. My eyes were closed, my attention directed inward, as tears escaped and trickled slowly down my cheeks. Tom has a wonderful voice that proclaimed the beauty of a song of love toward a heavenly Father, delivered by a good friend around the glow of the campfire. God's presence was palpable that night at McKeen Brook. This is the song he proclaimed in the wilderness:

> I can't believe you died for me
> You came to be, my sin, my shame
> You died for me so willingly.
>
> How can it be you chose someone like me
> To represent you in this world
> To sing your praises to those who can not see,
> and sing to you through all eternity.

I can't believe your love for me I did not earn,
You died for me—on that cross
I can't believe you loved me so.

You came to be, my sin, my shame
You died for me, so willingly
How can it be—that I see?
This joy, this grace, is all for me.

In my tent, as I settled into my warm sleeping bag, I thought more about Tom's testimony, the harmonica song and Psalm 139. How did God find me in the woods? I was utterly lost. But in that moment, I began to believe that God truly does search me and know me. He perceives my thoughts from afar and discerns my going out and my lying down and is familiar with all my ways. The song brought tears and the terrifying partridge experience had challenged my faith. I was amazed at how I was led from my self-made predicament by a partridge—most often a timid bird that flees from humans.

I also related to what I had read in Thomas Merton's book, *He Is Risen*, earlier that week, where he describes how we encounter God in the wilderness of life. It struck me intensely that I was now in the middle of the Allagash Wilderness. Merton encourages us, "True encounters with Christ liberate something in us, a power we did not know we had, a hope, a capacity for life, a resilience, an ability to bounce back when we thought we were completely defeated, a desire to grow and change."[1] What an overpowering, life-changing experience. Earlier in the day, I had faced fear in the woods, felt what it was like to be completely defeated, and then had a mysterious encounter with Christ.

---

1. Merton, *He Is Risen*, 2.

2

Harvard Medical School—Sort of
1978

IN THE LATE SEVENTIES, I embarked on a new chapter—a career in radiation therapy. Though often misunderstood by family and friends, this work was driven by an overpowering sense of purpose. Conversations about my job frequently faltered when the word "cancer" surfaced, reflecting the deep discomfort many felt even discussing the topic. The stigma around cancer was pervasive; people associated it with a death sentence and feared it as a terrible, incurable disease. The "C" word was seldom spoken. The mere mention of it seemed to suck the air out of the room, as though speaking its name would summon the disease itself. Yet, despite the unease it evoked in others, my interest in working with cancer patients was more than just a job; it became a well-paved road I traveled each day to touch lives and push the boundaries of cancer management. The work was challenging and often difficult, but fulfilling, as it allowed me to support those battling the disease and contribute to the slow and steady advancements in cancer treatment. Together, we were moving the needle toward curing more and more patients, especially those with breast and prostate cancer.

The journey began at a small freestanding clinic in Providence, brought to life by Dr. Webber, a tall, handsome gentleman known for his signature bow tie, which partially concealed the marks of his own battle. His neck, oddly asymmetrical, told the story of radical surgery and survival. Meeting him, one could hardly ignore the scar that ran from just above his jaw, jaggedly down to an inch or two above his clavicle—a stark reminder of his past ordeal. He always met your gaze with compassion in his eyes, a window into a heart that had stared down the fear of death. Once a revered surgeon, he had embraced a new calling after his own bout with cancer—to treat and bring hope to other cancer patients. Unlike most radiation therapy facilities, which were integrated into vast complex hospital networks, this clinic stood independent, a beacon of hope free from bureaucratic chains.

His disassociation from the larger radiation oncology institute at a nearby hospital was a daring move, nothing short of audacious. My association with him began during my second year at the Community College of Rhode Island, where I earned a degree in radiography, known at the time as "x-ray technology." His wife and two grown children lived on the east side of Providence, several blocks from one another. One of his sons attended medical school at Brown University, where Dr. Webber had graduated at the top of his class many years earlier. He hired me part-time, guaranteed me ten hours of work each week, and allowed me the freedom to make my own hours as a college student, as long as each patient's shielding blocks were accurately constructed, tested, and ready for their first day of treatment.

The physics staff taught me step by step how to use the heated combination of several metals, including lead and cadmium, to create the customized shielding blocks needed for each patient undergoing radiation therapy treatment. I began by examining their x-rays, carefully tracing the anatomy that the physician had outlined on the radiograph with a wax pencil. This slow, deliberate process created the mold, which received the warm, silver-looking metal. After the blocks were set and hardened, I would then secure them to a Plexiglas tray, labeled with the patient's name and the direction the tray should be inserted into the radiation treatment unit. It was essential the tray, some weighing up to twenty-five pounds, be positioned precisely in the treatment unit before the high-intensity radiation beam began to interact powerfully and invisibly with the fast growing cancer cells. This part-time job was a great fit for my schedule, but more importantly, it opened the door of curiosity. I embraced the challenge.

Before this, I had spent two years at the University of Rhode Island (URI), in the southern part of the state. The campus, nestled among vast turf farms and ancient woods, breathed a long history through its old buildings. The mid-1800s roots of the school, initially an agricultural college, resonated with the legacy of the Land Grant Act, which opened doors for many to public higher education, providing more opportunities for people to earn a degree. For me, higher education was a vague concept until a few months before graduation.

I wasn't entirely sure what higher education meant until my guidance counselor pulled me into her office and asked, "So Dennis, what are your plans after you graduate?" I nervously looked down at the floor and said, "I haven't developed a plan yet." I was busy with my girlfriend Bonnie, smoking pot, and trying to improve my soccer skills. I also enjoyed working part-time at a golf course, where I could golf for free on Mondays, when the course was closed to members.

Strategizing on the spot, I mapped out a new plan, "My brother David had already been accepted to URI to study plant science, so let's try that." I loved the outdoors and was fascinated with the mysteries of nature and thought it would be a great fit. Almost everybody who applied to URI was accepted. I was one of those average students in high school, despite my drinking on weekends and becoming a member of the high-noon club—a lunch-time ritual of sharing a joint before heading back to afternoon classes. I figured out how to study just enough to get by and not draw too much attention. Life was busy trying to establish oneself in the world of sports, along with a car and a girlfriend.

Sports always provided a significant source of motivation for me. My athleticism and quickness allowed me to excel on the field despite my small stature, which not only fueled my competitive spirit but also provided a sense of accomplishment that my fragile ego demanded. The thrill of competition pushed me continuously to improve, while the camaraderie with my teammates created a sense of belonging and mutual support. Each game and practice session was an opportunity to prove myself. Gaining respect, and experiencing the joy of shared victories and the hard lessons learned from defeat was a motivator. I hungered for the slaps on the back and the high-fives after a stunning performance on the soccer field. I had a few. My view of the world was shaped somewhat by my athletic ability—if I did well in sports, I would be appreciated, liked, and accepted.

I'd also developed a knack for making some spending money in addition to my job at the golf course by selling small amounts of weed to my friends and their friends. Using some of the skills I developed from selling shellfish and golf balls when I was younger, I would buy a fairly large quantity of marijuana, usually a pound of the rich-smelling flowering herb, divide it up by weighing smaller amounts into baggies, and then sell those smaller amounts to friends and others. The money was good, and at the time, I thought the risk was extremely low. I tried to avoid selling weed on school property. Unfortunately, I smoked a good deal of my profits.

That fall, when my brother and I arrived at URI, we shared a room together in the centrally located Butterfield Hall, which was connected to one of three campus cafeterias. David, the tallest of the five boys, stood in stark contrast to my shorter stature. His longer, narrow face was accentuated by a pronounced nose, sturdy brow, and remarkably clear skin—he had very little acne. He had a well-built physique, a testament to his active lifestyle. But, his choice of attire often leaned towards the disheveled, giving him a carefree look. David had a peculiar after-school routine that perfectly captured his absent-minded nature. He would sometimes come home, prepare a snack or put a Pop-Tart in the toaster, then turn on the TV, only to head outside to shoot baskets. More often than not, he would forget all about the toaster and the TV. This pattern of behavior was so typical of him that it became a familiar scene we would tease him about.

The well-worn older brick dormitory showed its scars from housing so many young, promising learners over the years. We would often try to guess what was cooking by the scents escaping from the kitchen below. I hardly ever went hungry, except if we stayed on campus during the weekend. We could only afford the five-day meal plan. Mom usually sent us back to school Sunday night with a dozen or so homemade meatballs jammed into an old Maxwell House coffee can. Dad even pulled some strings that first semester and obtained a small student loan from our local bank, making us feel momentarily rich (in debt, that is).

We had additional roommates connected by an adjoining door between the two rooms and agreed to keep the door open, signaling our desire for camaraderie. One roommate was more like David—focused, studied regularly, and was fun to be around. The other roommate, who flunked out after the first year, was more like me—partied too much and didn't put the needed time and effort into studying. We often got high together and then worked on our pool game.

Unsure of what I wanted to do with my life, I had other things on my mind besides studying and writing papers. My girlfriend Bonnie, learning to drink beer effectively, and selling enough pot to make some spending money occupied my time. I remember my brother getting awkwardly nervous, especially that first semester, whenever a pound of weed was divided up into small one-ounce bags, weighing each one with the little handheld scale kept hidden in a drawer under my shirts. David often looked at me intensely and said, "Dennis, this isn't cool . . . we're going to get caught. You know we could go to jail for this—both of us. We're definitely going to get kicked out of school." None of that ever happened. But it could have.

After two years of increasing financial strains, restlessness and recurring thoughts of marrying Bonnie, I decided to drop out and get married. Just after the wedding, we found a small summer rental on Narragansett Bay, our sanctuary until the warm winds of spring drove us out. Renting this beach house by the week would increase substantially if we stayed past May.

Bonnie's stunning beauty and quiet presence made her a natural candidate for a modeling career, but beneath her radiant exterior were real fears and small wounds. She had established a professional portfolio but was still waiting for a break. Growing up, she had witnessed the troubles and hardships of her parents' marriage, likely leaving her with some lingering fears of abandonment. Her father's departure had shaken her, instilling an underlying anxiety that those she loved might also leave.

Bonnie's fear of change was something she hid well, creating familiar routines and making new situations daunting. She usually thrived in the comfort of the known, where life's patterns provided a sense of control and security. Alterations to her carefully constructed patterns, whether big or small, might unsettled her. Alongside this, her aversion to confrontation made it difficult for her to voice her needs and desires, leading her to avoid disagreements, often at the expense of her own happiness. Despite these fears, Bonnie's heart yearned for love and companionship, seeking the deep emotional connection she desired.

In the modeling world, Bonnie saw a chance to express herself artistically and seek the attention she believed would complete her. The industry sometimes allowed her to channel her creativity through artistic dress, fashion, and photo shoots, providing an outlet for her emotions and a platform to showcase her outer beauty. Outwardly, Bonnie was stunningly beautiful, captivating everyone who met her with her small, round face adorned with tiny, delicate features. Her bright blue eyes sparkled with life, and her slender body was complemented by her long, dark brown hair. Inwardly, she feared being left alone or deserted by loved ones, likely due in part to her parents' divorce.

While at our beach house, she commuted to Providence with a friend, and I found a job that helped pay the bills. The dead-end job at the local dry cleaners became unbearable and physically challenging for me, drawing me toward higher education—this time at the community college. The anatomy and physiology course at URI had sparked a hidden interest and fascination with the human body and the bones that provided its invisible structure. During the interviews at the community college and hospital, I promised to cut my shoulder-length ponytail if accepted into the radiography program, thrilled by this new opportunity. Growing my hair long was an inward sign of my rebellion beginning in high school. This "cut" would become a huge sacrifice for me, marking a change in identity, direction and focus.

Leaving our beach house in May, Bonnie and I moved back to Barrington, securing a second-floor apartment above Bonnie's sister and brother-in-law. I thrived in the summer and fall semesters. Even my downstairs brother-in-law's frequent pot-smoking sessions couldn't distract me. To everyone's surprise, and more importantly mine, I had accumulated a very high grade-point-average upon graduation. Sensing a newfound ability ignited within me, I desired to uncover the mysteries of the powerful invisible rays and their interactions within the human body. I was eager to apply my skills.

I quickly integrated into the team at Radiation Oncology Associates, my first real full-time job after two long, demanding years earning an Associate's Degree. The clinic buzzed with activity, treating over fifty patients a day. Beverly, my boss, was a constant source of encouragement. Her leadership and incredible listening skills guided us, and her history with Dr. Webber at the old hospital made her the glue holding us all together. Patients and staff loved her.

Under Dr. Webber's and Beverly's mentorship, I grew in my understanding of the precision needed in radiation therapy to eradicate tumors while protecting healthy tissue. Our toolkit included accurate patient positioning, personalized imaging, and various shielding methods. The intricate treatment plans often required up to six beam angles, and with the physics team, I developed a template blocking system that added to precise treatment. Dr. Webber's admiration was an unspoken reward, a nod of approval that fueled my inner drive and dedication. This was another example of my "performance orientation" promoting an inaccurate image of who I thought I was inside. My ego loved it.

An unexpected opportunity arose when Beverly, on the planning board of the New England Radiation Therapy Conference that year, needed a replacement speaker, as one had backed out weeks before the conference. Nervous but excited, I presented my template blocking system to a small audience. The response was enthusiastic—the magnification formula at the core of my system made it easy to adapt an accurate patient shielding process in any clinic, and more importantly, it was extremely reproducible.

Dr. Webber encouraged me to take the next step and earn my national certification in radiation therapy. This meant more school. He was a respected leader in his profession and a great source of encouragement for me. I saved the glowing recommendation letter he meticulously wrote for me for some time. I would later take it out and read it when I was feeling down or discouraged. My ego liked all the positive things he recorded on paper. His signature and the Radiation Oncology Associates logo positioned in the top corner of the letter gave it weight.

The letter, along with my college transcripts, tipped the scales for acceptance into the Boston program. I later learned that scores of applicants applied for the five positions at Harvard's Joint Center for Radiation Therapy. All applicants were required to have national radiography certification and one year's work experience at a cancer center. I was in.

June 1980 marked the start of my sixty-mile journey to Boston each day, stretching into long hours of classes and long frustrating days of commuting. The practicality of a small dumpy apartment in Roxbury became evident—walking distance from Harvard Medical School and most of the five Boston hospitals comprising the Joint Center for Radiation Therapy. The apartment, shared with Aiden, a hard-working radiation therapy student, was a crash course in city living—cockroaches, mice everywhere, and the constant hum of sirens. Boston's Mission Hill district housed our battered brick building's third-floor apartment, which comprised two small rooms and a communal bathroom, which was shared among four other similar apartments on the third floor. The smell of cramped city living on a hot day was particularly noticeable. I brought along my bike with its metallic blue paint job to help move around the city. It made it easier to get around the crowded busy streets of Boston. In addition, I could also take the "T" (Boston's mass transit system), as my apartment building was located within walking distance to the Green Line.

Absent were mirrors in the shared bathroom, encouraging us to shave in our rooms each morning. It reminded me of an era long ago, evoking images of cowboys lathering their faces in front of a broken mirror and a small bowl of warm murky water on the dresser. Aiden and I took turns. The hot water for the shower must have been on a timer, as it ran lukewarm, then cold, after just a few short minutes. We adjusted. My new living arrangements meant being away from Bonnie four nights a week, anticipating we would see each other most every weekend.

Aiden grew up in northern Massachusetts, about the same distance from Boston as I was from Providence. He was in his late twenties, with a stocky build and a few extra pounds on his waist. He too had an x-ray background and was happy to be in the Harvard radiation therapy program.

Weekly gatherings at the Long Street Pub, not far our apartment, bonded the five radiation therapy students, and our shared experiences—eventually weaving a tight-knit community. The girls lived in the dorm, where male visitors were not permitted. The pub was small and poorly lit but provided three large booths, one large enough to accommodate the five of us on Thursdays. Paychecks, which was really a small stipend provided by the program, brought welcomed celebrations. Our weekends often found many of us working part-time in Boston to make ends meet or traveling back home to one of the New England states.

The Joint Center for Radiation Therapy, a collaboration between Harvard Medical School, area hospitals, and the Dana-Farber Cancer Institute, was a unique innovation in radiation oncology. They were moving the needle toward higher cure rates and fewer side effects from radiation treatment in many areas. The radiation biology lab, complete with a variety of experimental animals fascinated me. Much of what we engaged in that year would morph into state-of-the-art treatment throughout the United States and abroad, particularly in the demanding and complex anatomical area of breast cancer. In that era, radical mastectomies and partial mastectomies were the norm for breast cancer treatment, each an effective but severe measure to remove cancer cells along with potentially positive lymph nodes. We would become world-renowned in developing a pioneering technique to treat a patient's intact breast (instead of mastectomy) with high-dose radiation therapy after a surgical procedure called a lumpectomy; chemotherapy was added if needed. Collaboration among the various modalities was essential.

Simultaneously, an army of pediatric patients from all parts of the country and some from overseas waged their brave battles at our center too, often navigating the complexities of a combination of surgery, radiation, and chemotherapy at the Sidney-Farber Cancer Institute. We stood as a symbol of hope and innovation, one of a few referral centers for rare pediatric tumors.

That year in Boston flew by, and job offers poured in for everyone, as the shortage of radiation therapists intensified. The hospital in Castro Valley, California, captivated me with its dedicated professionals and scenic location. Married for four years with no children, we were willing to take the leap. California's land of opportunity promised increased advancement for both of us and a new beginning in a far away land.

Bonnie updated her portfolio of images in hopes of landing a modeling career out of San Francisco. She, however, was somewhat apprehensive about the move, uncertain about finding work in a big city and making new friends. She was deeply connected to her family and friends, especially her two sisters, who lived close by. The thought of leaving them and her mother behind probably filled her with a mix of anxiety and fear. I encouraged her every chance I could. One evening, as we sat watching TV, she confided, "I know this is a big change for us, and I'm excited for you. With your new job—they really seem to like you—but California is so far away. You know, the whole idea gives me an ache right here. Although, I am looking forward to driving cross-country." I squeezed her hand, gratitude surging. "We'll make some great memories, just like we have here," I assured her. "And we'll always have family to come back to. Think of the weather in San Francisco—no snow."

Packing up our belongings, each item carried a story, a memory of our life on the east coast. The move was a leap into the unknown, but we were doing it together. A promising full-time job in radiation therapy, with overtime available, awaited me. We were young, childless, and eager to take on the world, armed with our U-Haul trailer, each other's support, and the promises of the San Francisco bay area.

As the last weeks of our move approached, Bonnie gave her two-week notice at the insurance company, where she had traveled each day with my brother. Wayne was working in another department, and he and Bonnie commuted back and forth over a period of about two years, primarily while I was in Boston. He was unhappy, forced to travel to Providence solo for the rest of that year after losing his commuting buddy to California. We sold or gave away most possessions, keeping only what fit in the small U-Haul trailer. Tying a few items outside on the trailer, we traveled coast to coast swiftly. I needed to pass two exams in Sacramento to start work at the hospital. We had eight days to get there.

We arrived two days ahead of schedule, taking northern US Route 80 through Cleveland, Des Moines, Cheyenne and Salt Lake City before settling into a campground just outside of Sacramento, located on the west branch of the American River. This would give me the needed time to review for the exams. I remember the wild turkeys, deer, and beautiful flowers near the campground. It was absolutely stunning scenery. Each day was warm, full of sun and packed with excursions. One day we panned for gold, and another we enjoyed running the small river rapids over and over on rented tubes. The water was fast moving and refreshing.

Both exams went well. I felt good about my responses. I would be allowed to work at the hospital pending the test results.

Things seemed to be falling into place after arriving in Castro Valley. Work was demanding, but rewarding.

The emotional changes we experienced moving from the east coast, combined with the additional stresses of finding an apartment were more than we anticipated. The weather in the area didn't change much—it was the same sunny blue skies most every day. One day blurred into the next with little if any rain, and temperatures perpetually in the eighties. The relentless wind blew daily, growing stronger as the day progressed. Without it, the heat would be unbearable, making air conditioning essential. Our new apartment had it, along with a community swimming pool, but even these comforts couldn't shake Bonnie's growing sense of discontent. Some days we could smell the delicious aroma of chocolate from the factory near our apartment complex. Other days, depending on which way the wind was blowing, brought a fine mist of furniture dust from a small factory two blocks away. What a mess if one forgot to close the windows.

As the weeks passed, I could sense she wasn't especially happy. She felt too nervous to venture over to San Francisco to look for modeling work. Her enthusiasm waned, and she started to withdraw from me and talk more and more on the phone to her sisters. I thought it would pass; we settled into our new surroundings.

The move to California began to take its toll on our relationship. Bonnie's longing for the familiar east coast mirrored her deeper, unspoken questions about our new life and continued relationship. As the days passed, I couldn't ignore the growing tension between us. We weren't fighting—we were just growing apart. The calm exterior of our sunny west-coast life was about to be challenged by the unseen winds of change.

After much discussion, Bonnie, uncomfortable with flying, decided to take an eastbound Amtrak from Oakland to Providence in late August—a journey that would take about four days passing through Chicago. After arriving back in Barrington, she planned to stay with her mother and younger sister to sort things out. We had both agreed this was a trial separation, giving us each time to evaluate our relationship. She knew before moving out west that it would be difficult living so far away from family. I was more settled, as I had developed several relationships at work. She had very few friends in Castro Valley and was still looking for the right job in San Francisco.

The long train ride gave her time to reflect and think. Was her marriage going to work? How much did she miss her family and friends in Rhode Island? Unspoken issues lingered. As I waved goodbye on the train platform, a profound emptiness settled within me, a restlessness I couldn't shake. Unbeknownst to me, Bonnie had fallen in love with another, and our sunny Californian adventure grew dark. Something in my heart felt odd about what happened that day—a strange hollowness began to expand and remained with me for some time.

3

Secrets Unraveled
1981

I WAS ABOUT TO be tested in a way I had never anticipated. It was the day before Thanksgiving when the phone rang—a call that would shake me to my core. After several months into our trial separation, Bonnie had something urgent to discuss—something she had scarcely shared with anyone.

From the moment I heard her voice, I sensed her unease. She was nervous about something, troubled, and somewhat cautious. Our conversation was riddled with awkward pauses, the love and care that once defined us noticeably absent. My heart sank as I thought, "Maybe she was going to tell me we were drifting apart more than I thought—after just four short years of marriage."

She spoke haltingly about her feelings and the growing distance between us. Her words confirmed what I had feared—we were miles apart, both physically and emotionally. I knew I wasn't the perfect husband and couldn't shake the guilt that gnawed at me for not trying harder to bridge the gap. Perhaps if I had paid more attention to her needs instead of my own wants and desires, things would be different. One of us was on the west coast, the other on the east, and our weekly phone calls were a desperate attempt to bridge the chasm that had formed. The past year had been especially tough on our marriage, but nothing had prepared me for the revelation Bonnie was about to share.

We had just sold everything we had earlier that year to move to California. My new employer agreed to pay me twice the amount I was offered for two similar jobs in New England, one at Dr. Webber's clinic. Granted, the cost of living was much higher in California.

Up to this point, I had been in and out of school for about half of the four years we were married, living mostly on Bonnie's income as the breadwinner from her Aetna Insurance job. The year before moving to California, I was commuting home most weekends while I studied and worked part-time at the Dana-Farber Cancer Institute every other weekend.

Fortunately, we then lived in an upstairs apartment owned by her mother and stepfather. Her sister lived on the first level. This reduced our living expenses and provided Bonnie with some companionship while I was in Boston Monday through Thursday.

The phone call that day would change my life forever. She tried to explain that she had fallen out of love some time ago. Things with us were different—we had grown apart. Her love had been captured by someone else, and they would be moving into an apartment together on the west side of Providence.

What was I hearing? She was so sorry. She didn't mean to hurt me. Before she could finish, I could feel the pain grip me and the tears begin to form. My throat tightened and pulse quickened. The shock of the news sent my nervous system into overdrive as my body struggled to cope.

Discovering that I had been tossed aside for another inflicted a searing pain that cut deep into the core of my being. It was like drinking a nasty cocktail of betrayal, bitter heartbreak, and shattered trust. It tasted awful. I grappled with negative thoughts and agonizing questions about my self-worth. The chatter in my brain amplified. It was an emotional pain that I knew would lead to a good deal of anxiety and long-lasting trust issues. Speechless, I readied myself for more pain that was on the way.

A long, uncomfortable silence hung between us. Bonnie, attempting to hold back tears, sobbed and confessed what she had been hiding for some time. "It's your brother Wayne," she confessed quietly, her voice breaking. She grew more uncomfortably silent after a long pause, unable to continue. "But how could this be?" I stammered, feeling a surge of confusion and gripping anger. "What do you mean, Bonnie?" She took a deep breath, her voice trembling. "I didn't know how to tell you. I didn't want to hurt you."

My mind raced. Memories of Wayne flashed before me—his laughter, his kindness in looking after Bonnie while I was in Boston. "Why didn't you tell me sooner?" I asked, my voice barely above a whisper. "We could have . . . we could have done something." Bonnie's sobbing grew louder, as she said, "I was scared. I didn't know . . . I didn't know how you would react. And then, as time went on, it became harder and harder to say anything at all." I felt a mix of confusion and sadness, saying, "Bonnie, we're supposed to be honest with each other. Why would you think keeping this from me would be better?" "I thought I was protecting you," she defended, her voice barely a whisper. "But I realize now that I was wrong. I'm so sorry."

The weight of her words hung heavily in the air. The long silence was becoming increasingly awkward. I struggled to process everything I was hearing on the phone, and the deep pain that gripped me. "What exactly happened with Wayne?" I asked, my voice growing louder and my heart pounding harder. The world felt like it was collapsing around me. Wayne . . . my brother, and Bonnie? I felt an overwhelming sense of confusion and bitterness. "Why, Bonnie? Why Wayne?" Bonnie's sobs grew louder. "I know. I know. I'm so sorry. I thought I was doing the right thing, but I see now that I was wrong. Please, forgive me."

I grew very quiet—my mind racing in a whirlwind of emotions as we prepared to say goodbye. The ending of this traumatic conversation was uncomfortable for both of us. She piped in and said, "We can talk more about all this next week. I am so sorry, Dennis."

Wayne was gay. At least that is what he claimed to be since he was in high school, and maybe even before then. Bonnie and Wayne? They had commuted together for years at Aetna. Wayne always demonstrated a kind-heartedness and generosity that was evident to those who knew him. I was aware that they were good friends, as they hung out a lot together, especially while I was in Boston. I thought my brother was looking after her for me. Maybe this was where they had shared their hearts with each other and began to think about a future together. She explained on the phone that Wayne might not actually be gay. They had somehow fallen in love. Wayne was seriously questioning his sexuality. He actually thought it might be better to be with his sister-in-law than to be gay.

He related a story where, some time earlier, our older brother, who was newly focused on following Jesus and his teachings, had been praying for him not to be gay. The thinking at the time was that Wayne had made an earlier decision in his life to be gay and could now make a new decision not to be gay. Surely some intense prayer on a weekend retreat in Maine would do the trick, his brother thought. After Don bailed him out of an unexpected financial jam while he was in Maine on a long weekend with friends, Wayne promised to go on the weekend retreat. I am not sure what happened on the retreat, but it apparently left Wayne very confused about his sexuality. This whole thing sounded like a soap opera script, with pain, betrayal, and romance all oddly woven together.

Wayne, just shy of six feet tall, carried himself with an understated style that reflected his artistic nature. His trim figure was often accentuated by trendy clothes, as he loved to shop, spending his money on items that brought him joy—whether it was an expensive new pair of slacks, a distinctive cologne, or a unique treasure that caught his eye.

The youngest of five boys, he grew up with a unique sense of rejection that still lingered, perhaps stemming from his mother's plan to try for a girl and his father's dismissal of him for being gay when he attempted to come out of the closet. Despite these challenges, he focused his inventive talents on everything he did, both in his work and in his personal style.

Later that day, after the shocking phone call, the confusion of this new information began to penetrate deeper and deeper. Reality set in. I felt nauseous and sick, foolish for not suspecting the infidelity. The bitterness of betrayal gripped me. I was emotionally upset and wanted to get far away, to run and hide from humanity and my new problem. Facing the news felt overwhelming, triggering waves of apprehension and anxiety. Isolation seemed like the only way to avoid the emotional strain of confronting my new reality.

When she left on the Amtrak out of Oakland, she tried to explain, "The real reason for our trial separation was due to the move to California, Dennis. It had left me feeling so lonely and missing my family and friends back east." That may have been partly true.

What an idiot I was. Wayne was one of those "friends" she missed back east. I remember the scene on the train platform. It was right out of an old movie where two people are saying goodbye, one peering down from the window of the train and the other walking along the platform, as the huge double-decker train moved slowly out of town. She waved from the window high above, and I walked slowly along the platform, waving goodbye, and then stood still for quite some time, feeling empty and alone as she moved out of sight, heading eastbound out of my life.

The engine exhaust from the train drifted down onto the platform, carrying a distinctive odor heavy with the smell of burnt fuel and oil. As I inhaled deeply, the taste was bitter and unpleasant, leaving a lingering sensation in my throat and mouth. The overall experience on the platform was disturbing and overwhelming. A middle-aged woman approached me on the almost empty platform, placing her hand on my shoulder and gently shaking me back to reality, saying, "Are you okay? Hey, are you okay? Did you lose somebody? Can I help you find them?" Over the next several months, I was in a deep stupor—disconnected from relationships.

4

Forgive Us Our Debts
1981

PACKING MY TENT, CAMPING gear, and enough food and clothes for several days, I set out on a spur-of-the-moment trip to Yosemite National Park. It was a temporary escape, a chance to clear my head. I was told Yosemite was one of the most visited national parks in the country, full of incredible beauty, majesty, and the unknown. It was Thanksgiving Day, and I was not very thankful. This trip, I thought, would provide a good opportunity to get away and clear my head. Yosemite is a challenging three-hour drive almost directly east from Castro Valley, nestled on the western slopes of the Sierra Nevada Mountains. My truck was built for this journey.

Yosemite's landscape ranges from foothills to alpine crags, and I was eager to explore iconic spots like Half Dome, El Capitan, and Yosemite Point. A setting like this translates into fantastic scenery for my camera, especially on the valley floor, located about four thousand feet above sea level. One of my patients told me earlier that week that President Kennedy had visited the park in 1962 and stayed at the historic Ahwahnee Hotel located in the valley and that Marilyn Monroe was also at the hotel that week. This raised lots of questions in the press about adultery and infidelity.

The pricey hotel was also on my bucket list, built in the 1920s as a luxury retreat for wealthy travelers, who wanted to experience the beauty and majesty of the park, and avoid the pitfalls of camping. The altitude of Yosemite, which ranged from a few thousand feet to over thirteen thousand feet, did not concern me, as my twin brother and I had climbed most of the four thousand-foot-plus peaks in the White Mountains of New Hampshire during our Boy Scout years, some on snowshoes.

While true altitude sickness is usually an issue for folks heading for high summits above five thousand feet, I learned that some can experience mild symptoms from smaller elevation changes, such as headaches, tiredness, and loss of appetite. Interestingly, I had been experiencing many of these symptoms at sea level before departing on my trip to the park. Arriving at Yosemite was another challenge I had not planned for or expected.

After reaching the western park entrance at Big Oak Flat Visitor Center, the ranger greeted me: "Welcome. How are you doing today? Do you have chains for your truck to enter the park, as it is snowing at higher elevations?" Shocked, I responded, "No, I don't have any chains." He calmly replied, "Your best bet is to head back to Groveland and buy a set. There's a hardware store that should be open until eight." Disappointed, I thanked him and asked, "How far is Groveland from here?"

I wasn't familiar with tire chains or how to install them. Did I need two or four? I would soon find out after traveling the thirty-two miles back to Groveland and locating the hardware store in town. Just as the ranger said, they were open and had plenty of chains to choose from. This store must do good business selling chains; there were plenty to choose from. All I needed was the numbers on the side of my sixteen-inch tire—*Off-Road: 265/70R16*. I was grateful they were open on Thanksgiving Day.

My escape-from-reality adventure took an unexpected twist after I arrived back at the Big Oak Flat park entrance and attempted to put the chains on my tires. Three of the four fit perfectly—one was too small. An oversight at the factory late on a Friday afternoon? This meant traveling back to Groveland again to get a replacement set of chains. After arriving at the hardware store and getting the new box of chains, I wanted to make sure they actually did fit. I put them on right there in front of the hardware store, where there was no accumulated snow. They fit. After removing the chains and putting them back in the box, it was back to the park entrance. I found myself frustrated in a real proving ground.

In life's spiritual journey, trials often come our way, testing us. Moments like this one challenged my patience and inner strength. I still didn't like that amidst this challenge, growth would take root and I would become stronger. Arriving at the valley floor near the hotel well after sunset, with the snow still coming down, I chose to sleep with my grief in the cab of my truck that night. It was much colder than I expected, even with a good sleeping bag. Over fourteen inches of snow had accumulated by morning, translating into a winter wonderland of beauty and solitude. It created a stillness all around me—a quietness both inside and out that was hard to describe. The distant hum of a motor vehicle could be heard, breaking the silence. To my utter amazement, the rangers were quick to open the roads.

After the storm, I discovered peace and solitude were by my side that morning among the spectacular scenery surrounding me. The fresh fallen snow made it feel like a new day, clean and full of beauty. Everything was covered in a pure coat of whiteness, limbs bowing low. With my camera in hand, I took dozens of shots, using my telephoto lens, of waterfalls surrounding mountain peaks and a memorable scene on the valley floor. It perfectly captured the essence of my mood.

Before me lay a small clearing, about seventy-five yards wide, with five or six large hardwood trees scattered in the foreground. The fresh snow covered the entire area. A dense row of smaller pines formed a thick semi-circular border toward the back of the scene, giving way to a misty fog that obscured the tall mountains barely visible behind. Off to the side stood a lone tree, broken off about forty feet above the snow level. It sat all alone. The remains of the naked tree exposed a few small remnants of broken branches, perhaps the result of another storm. I, too, felt just like that tree—broken and alone.

Surrounded by God's creation, I recalled the Bible verse I had studied some weeks ago: "Come now, let us reason together, says the Lord; though your sins are like scarlet, they shall be as white as snow" (Isa 1:18). God can accomplish what seems impossible for us to achieve on our own. A cloth, dyed red stays red. As hard as we try, we cannot make the cloth white again. But regardless of the stain of our sins, the sacrifice of God's son can make us clean again. I contemplated Jesus' sacrifice, knowing that when I stand before God in judgment, he will see me through the purity of Jesus, like freshly fallen snow. Not red but white as snow. It was a revelation in my heart, assuring me I was loved and forgiven.

When I returned to work on Monday, I spoke to one of the chaplains at the hospital, Fr. John, about my experience at Yosemite and the strange sense of a "presence" even in my grief and loneliness. Father John, who often helped us transfer patients from their hospital beds to stretchers for transport to the radiation therapy department, said, "There are many beliefs about how God communicates with people. In some, God speaks to us through nature. This can take all kinds of forms, such as experiencing a sense of peace and connection to something greater than us, like a sunset or while spending time in the woods, like you did at Yosemite. Or it can be finding a sign or messages from God in the natural world. Some believe that they can distinctly feel the presence of God in the outdoors. Other times it may be a friend or relative that provides spiritual insight. Pain can come in many forms and often takes us by surprise," Father John continued.

As I reflected on what he was saying, I was reminded of my roommate Jeff's death. What a shocking event. Here one day— gone the next—at twenty-five years old. It stunned all of us late one night when his motorcycle was found in a canyon just off Lake Chabot Road, less than a mile from our shared apartment. Witnesses reported him speeding and failing to negotiate a sharp turn in the road, flying through the air nearly thirty-five feet before landing among some large boulders in the canyon below. Two nurses I knew from the emergency room at the hospital didn't think it was a good idea for me to be the one to identify the body, although I wanted to help. I was gently turned away.

Everyone loved Jeff. He had a charismatic smile and an excitement about life. He was a great roommate—just what I needed after my separation. The pain remained for a long time, even after his funeral in Delaware. I was pleasantly surprised that Bonnie joined me to help in mourning the death of my close friend.

Father John wrapped up our conversation by reminding me, "It's important to note that people have different experiences and interpretations of how God speaks to them and that there is no one-size-fits-all answer to the question." I was beginning to understand one way that God speaks to us: through our pain.

5

AC/DC
1982

JULIE NAMED HER CAT "DC" to keep Jeff's memory alive, as he was a big fan of the rock band AC/DC. She had one cat for me and one for her. We were all still in shock, mourning his passing, especially after attending his funeral in Delaware. Jeff was full of life and adventure, and his death was a tremendous blow. I had never lost anyone that close to me at such a young age. I had just seen him earlier that day.

The night after Jeff's death, we all gathered together to trade stories and help each other process the loss of our twenty-five-year-old friend. We petitioned the local radio station to dedicate a song by Lynyrd Skynyrd, and now whenever "Free Bird" plays, I remember my good friend. The disc jockey chose the longer ten-minute version to make it special and help us through our grief. We cried together mourning his death, which was a shock for all of us who knew him.

Jeff loved rock music, and everyone knew that. When AC/DC toured in northern California, they scheduled three back-to-back shows at the fourteen-thousand-seat Cow Palace in San Francisco, and Jeff attended all of them. He said it was the greatest concert series he had ever been to. The volume was so loud that he had to roll up matchbook covers to use as earplugs; he still couldn't hear well for several days afterward. The show opened with "Hells Bells" as the lead singer pounded a large bell with a big sledgehammer. He couldn't get enough of the music or the lead singer, Brian Johnson. The Australian band planned to continue their tour and travel to Denver for two shows later that week. If Jeff had enough funds, he might have traveled to Colorado.

Jeff started working at the hospital delivering supplies, shuttling packages and equipment to various departments, with particular focus on the operating room, emergency room, and the radiation therapy department. It was during these hospital deliveries that our paths crossed and we got to know each other. Jeff quickly engaged in conversations filled with banter, jokes, and discussions on topics ranging from football—especially the San Francisco 49ers—to where to eat good food. Liked by nearly everyone he encountered, Jeff's popularity extended throughout the hospital. With his long, blondish-brown hair typically tied back in a ponytail, he exuded the unmistakable aura of a rock guitarist.

Jeff had moved from Delaware to Castro Valley months earlier with his friends Mark and Delia, and their young child. He initially lived with them, helping with rent until he could secure his own apartment, which he did shortly after Bonnie left. When Jeff wasn't immersed in his hospital duties, he loved watching weekend football, his enthusiasm centered around Joe Montana and the San Francisco 49ers. Sundays turned into a small party with friends, featuring beer, camaraderie, and the ever-present scent of local cannabis. Jeff's outgoing personality drew people in, including me.

One unforgettable Sunday morning late in the football season, several months after we became roommates, Jeff unveiled a bold plan. He suggested we attend the National Football Conference Championship playoff game between the 49ers and their archrivals, the Dallas Cowboys. "It's a home game, and tickets will be a breeze to get," he exclaimed with unwavering confidence. Without a second thought, we prepared for the thirty-minute journey to San Francisco by car, filled with eagerness and anticipation.

My excitement was palpable as I would witness my first national football game in San Francisco at Candlestick Park.

The game unfolded with an intensity that electrified the stadium. Going into the second half of the game, the 49ers were trailing. Late in the fourth quarter, as time was running out, it happened—a moment that would forever be etched in our memories. Six-foot-four inch Dwight Clark, propelled by sheer determination, leapt high into the end zone above the defenders, miraculously catching the ball on his fingertips. The home-field crowd erupted in a thunderous roar. Dallas failed to score in the minute that remained. That iconic play, called "The Catch" replayed endless times on TV, and stands as a testament to the human spirit and the fierce intensity of the football playoffs. That catch thrust the 49ers into the Super Bowl, where they would later emerge triumphant over the Cincinnati Bengals.

I was there, caught in that whirlwind of emotion. The passion that coursed through my veins caused me to shout for the 49ers as loud as all those sitting around me, leaving me with a very sore throat for days thereafter. To this day, the experience of attending that game remains a cherished memory. It was a spontaneous idea born from Jeff's hunger for excitement and adventure—a reminder of his commitment to living life to the fullest. Jeff loved a good time.

With a hunger for thrills and excitement, Jeff and I discovered another unexpected camaraderie beyond the hospital walls. Our rendezvous took place every Friday evening at the Doucet Saloon in Castro Valley, a lively establishment known for its fusion of Venezuelan and Mexican cuisine. As the week drew to a close, we looked forward to our ritual of indulging in a cold beer and engaging in competitive games of pool. This weekly outing became an anticipated escape, surrounded by friendly competition. It was during those Friday nights that Julie, a delightful addition to our group, would occasionally join us.

Although Julie's skills on the pool table were average, her company was always welcome. Following our pool matches, we would sometimes convene at our apartment across the street from the hospital, where she would bring her laundry and a nice bottle of California red wine. She had a natural charm, hailed from the Golden State, and radiated genuine fondness for both Jeff and me. She was stunningly good looking, fun to be around, and liked to have a good time.

She worked at the hospital, single-handedly running the printing department. Preferring the convenience of our basement laundry facility over a crowded Laundromat, Julie would pamper us with her latest wine choice. On special occasions, she would even bring along "sensimilla," a more potent strain of marijuana cultivated exclusively in Humboldt County, California, farther north, near the Oregon border. Whenever Julie came over to do her laundry, we always knew we were in for a great evening. She introduced us to a number of first time experiences, including the new strain of weed whose smell was so distinct and inviting.

It was Julie who initiated me into the realm of fine red wine. As a good stock market investor and longtime employee at the hospital, she possessed an affinity for the finer things in life, including nice cuisine, stylish attire, and the allure of her hand polished red Corvette. Under Julie's tutelage, we embarked on a new journey, gradually acquainting ourselves with the diverse red wines produced in the nearby Napa and Sonoma Counties. These included cabernet sauvignon, merlot, and other finely crafted red blends.

One weekend, Julie invited Jeff and me to a wine tasting. The prospect excited us, as we yearned to learn and discern the qualities that set different red wines apart. Sometime later in my journey, I remembered this wine tasting event with a new insight. Embarking on a spiritual undertaking was similar to drinking a fine red wine. I thought that each sip of wine unveiled layers of flavor, from bold tannins to subtle hints of berries and oak. Each step of the journey revealed new depths of insight and enlightenment. Both required patience and an open mind to truly appreciate their complexities. And much like a good red wine, a spiritual adventure might leave me with a warm, lingering sense of fulfillment and a thirst for more.

Our group gathered at a well-worn curved oak bar adorned with six glasses and a scorecard for each participant. A knowledgeable wine expert guided us through the basics of evaluating the wine. The focal point was a series of six red cabernet sauvignon wines all from Napa County, presented in small pours. To truly appreciate the wine's qualities, we were advised to engage our senses—comparing the appearance of each glass, savoring its aroma, exploring its taste and texture. As a novice, I initially felt adrift, unsure of what to discern from all that was going on. Although, the experience created a thirst to learn.

Engrossed in this newfound passion, Jeff and I discovered that indulging in the art of drinking good wine transcended mere intoxication. Our new skill became a source of pride and a symbol of personal growth. As I immersed myself amidst the mid-range wines, a routine formed; shopping and asking questions about selecting the right bottle for the right occasion. Most of the time, I bought the wine because it tasted good.

My apartment, conveniently located across from the hospital, served as a gateway to my wine education. I would occasionally detour to The Chabot liquor store, which boasted a modest wine selection, mostly from California. This quarter-mile journey back to my two-story apartment would often find me carrying a couple bottles of red, eager to explore new flavors with Jeff and Julie. The store soon became a welcoming distraction, where I formed friendships with the two boys behind the counter and eventually purchased my first case of wine. Bonding over conversations about four-wheeling, football, and other adventures, Steve, the manager, encouraged me to open a tab, allowing me to settle my expenses at the end of the month.

During one visit, Steve extended an invitation to join their four-wheeling excursions on weekends. Initially hesitant to subject my new truck to potential dirt and damage, I eventually agreed. Our weekend adventures captured the spirit of exploration, as we sought to cover our trucks in mud without succumbing to its clutches. Amidst the revving engines and the camaraderie forged through shared beer, wine, and weed, we found ourselves fostering new friendships and the joy of the present moment. Although, getting the mud off my truck was an unwanted adventure.

As the seasons changed, different opportunities presented themselves with Steve and my new liquor store buddies. The boys at the store proposed that I join them and become the tenth partner in renting a ski lodge in Lake Tahoe for the upcoming winter season. Although I only knew three of the ten ski bums involved, the prospect of gambling on new friendships, rejuvenating my skiing skills, and escaping the clutches of my "Bonnie troubles" enticed me. Lake Tahoe would be exciting and a great place to explore.

With a willingness to embrace the snow covered mountains, I accepted the invitation to join the group. The rented lodge, nestled amidst the breathtaking beauty of Lake Tahoe, accommodated fourteen and was close to several renowned ski resorts, including Palisades.

The initial weekend at the lodge was calm, as some of the resorts had yet to open all their trails. However, as the season gained momentum, each passing weekend brought an influx of more friends and visitors, often exceeding the lodge's capacity. After an exciting day on the slopes, we reconvened at the lodge, indulging in beer and weed. Most of us drank from a pony keg of beer, smoked plenty of weed, and some snorted cocaine. Card games added an element of competition to the mix. It was Steve who introduced me to the pricey white powder. He would later develop a problem with it, causing him both physical and financial hardship.

The ski-lodge atmosphere brimmed with vibrant energy, including a diverse mix of attractive young women and some unfamiliar faces joining our snow-filled adventures each weekend. Securing a sleeping spot early in the evening became crucial, as the night grew longer and the party intensified, finding yourself dozing off in a chair or on the floor was an all too common occurrence.

On occasion, I would extend an invitation to Stan, a friend from the hospital, leaving San Francisco as early as possible on Friday after the workday's end. The thrill of the drive and the anticipation of our upcoming adventures fueled our spirits. Yet, as the weekend's adventure waned and the time came to bid farewell to the snow-capped peaks, my body and head would ache, wearied from the relentless pursuit of happiness. The three-and-a-half-hour drive back to Castro Valley on Sunday offered a period of quiet reflection.

Our conversations during these drives often ranged from deep reflections on life to light-hearted banter. "I can't believe how beautiful everything is from the top of the Ecstasy Trail. Such stunning views of Lake Tahoe," Stan would exclaim, glancing out the window. "Yeah, it was breathtaking." I'd reply, smiling and nodding in agreement. "The color of the dark blue-green lake contrasting with all the snow is remarkable. I took some great photos. Makes all the effort worth it." Sometimes, the conversation would take a more serious turn. "Do you ever think about what life is really about, like in the end?" Stan asked, his tone more serious. "I do . . . more now since my circumstances have changed. I feel like these trips to Tahoe help me figure things out a bit," I'd respond, appreciating the moment.

"You know, Stan, I think my skiing is getting better each time we hit the slopes," I mused. "I've finally perfected the art of stopping by digging the edges of my skis hard into the snow. Sometimes, I even manage to create a huge spray. Makes me feel like a pro." Stan laughed, "I noticed that. Especially when you almost sprayed that guy in the yellow parka on the last run of the day." "Yeah, that was stupid of me," I chuckled. "But it was fun. Getting to know some of the others in the group has also been a plus," I continued. "Jim and Cindy are continually sharing their faith with me on the chairlift. It's kind of nice to have those conversations up here. It feels like God's country." "They seem really engaged with us. And they're both intermediate skiers like us," Stan replied. "Yeah, I think you're right Stan, she's a bit better than him. So many of the others are either experts or at least trying to look like experts," I complained as I gazed out the window.

And as we arrived home, I appreciated the fact that I was not due at the hospital until nine o'clock. I was part of the second shift, which usually meant staying late, maybe until six o'clock. We had to make sure all the patients were treated and the new patients' treatment calculations were double checked and filed. I was the new boy on the block and didn't have a family to rush home to at the end of the workday. So, I stayed late welcoming the overtime.

Before finally wrapping up the weekend, it was customary to share a high-end joint from Doug's previous year's growth with whoever ended up at my apartment on a Sunday evening. Smoking weed and enjoying a nice glass of red became a routine I enjoyed. A bottle of red didn't last long on Sunday night or any other night for that matter. Hoping others would bring a bottle with them when they came over would be nice; especially Tim and Nancy. We labeled those two as "takers." Somehow, my apartment became the focal point of self-indulgence. Many of my new friends felt the same way. We were all wandering through life together in the wilderness, just like Moses and the Israelites, but at the time, we didn't even know we were wandering aimlessly.

The sensimilla weed I was buying from Doug was stretching my budget. It was the sticky, dense, seedless stuff from Northern California—the stuff Julie introduced us to. Because I knew Doug so well, I was expected to buy the limited edition weed from him for everyone else who also appreciated its high quality. As a result, I became the connector—the middle man. This arrangement worked financially for me. I later learned that Doug and his family grew the stuff up in Humboldt County. I wanted to learn more about the details of his "family operation."

6

Into the Green Unknown
1982

ROBIN AND DOUG, AN active and outgoing couple living in Redwood Canyon not too far from me, had become more than just friends. Our relationship evolved into a unique business partnership. Doug drove a good-looking car, played golf most weekends, and had nice clothes and furniture, along with a large hot tub we all enjoyed together.

They became my go-to source for high-quality marijuana. Over time, I cautiously purchased sizable quantities of the herb from them, always at their home. We didn't just conduct business transactions; we shared experiences. Doug and I bonded and competed together on the golf course. After golf, at his house, we would usually share some weed and perhaps a bottle of wine. I later discovered they were master growers who had reaped the benefits of multiple harvests. In fact, Robin's sister, brother-in-law, and even her middle-aged mother had been cultivating marijuana with them as a family enterprise. They were all involved in the business of growing and cultivating marijuana for big profit, and I was fascinated by the details. I wanted to know more. This interest of mine led to an unexpected invitation. Doug persuaded me to join them for the fall harvest.

It was in October that Randy and I began our thrilling journey to rendezvous with Doug and Robin and learn more about the harvest. Randy had traveled from Colorado at my invitation, joining me on our first-ever Humboldt County harvesting adventure. It was a time when both of us liked to party, usually with little concern for our responsibilities or the consequences of our self-indulgent lifestyle. Together, we embarked on a pleasure-seeking adventure, driving north in my trusty Toyota pickup.

"I can't believe we're doing this, can you?" I proclaimed to Randy as we pulled onto the highway. "Absolutely, I sure can," Randy replied, his eyes revealing his anticipation. "Where exactly are we headed?" "Our destination is a clandestine, secret location," I explained, my voice filled with intrigue. "I understand it's nestled between the mountains and forests, with huge valleys and flatlands used for growing all sorts crops. They grow everything from vegetables to marijuana up there." "Sounds like just the right place for hidden wonders," Randy said, leaning back in his seat, lighting a joint and taking a long drag. "It truly is," I agreed. "This place is known for its breathtaking beauty and stunning landscapes. Located on the northern Pacific coast, it has huge redwood forests, a rugged coastline, and several mountain ridges that I can't wait to explore."

As we drove north, the conversation flowed naturally, moving between plans for our adventure and reflections on life. "Will we have time to see those massive redwoods?" Randy mused. "I've heard they're like nothing else in the world. Some trees at the base are bigger than this truck." "Are they really?" I asked. "And the coastline is just as spectacular. Ragged, untamed, and absolutely mesmerizing." With every mile we traveled, the anticipation grew, and the unspoiled landscape unfolded before us mile after mile.

As we neared the end of our five-hour drive, the veil of darkness shrouded our arrival as we navigated our rendezvous with Doug at a small grocery store tucked away in an obscure rural part of the state. We followed strict security guidelines that Doug insisted on, well aware of the danger and numerous surrounding marijuana cultivation sites.

We parked about a hundred yards from the grocery store, now closed. Questions nagged us. Were we in the right place? Were we being followed? An air of tension hung in the still night, devoid of any activity except for dozens of flickering moths attracted to a solitary streetlight. We had ventured into a realm known for producing some of the finest high-quality marijuana in the country. The risks were real, and serious doubts crept in. After what seemed like an eternity, Doug finally showed up. He guided us through a labyrinth of locked gates and down a long, steep dirt road. I had to engage the 4-wheel drive, requiring a quick stop to lock the outside hubs of each wheel—old school technology.

Our journey ended in a small dirt parking area covered by trees and surrounded by large bushes, not far from a huge shed-like structure that would serve as our headquarters for the upcoming days. The dimly lit interior revealed a gathering of quintessential hippies—all related to Doug, happily trimming buds and engrossed in evening banter. The scene was set in a comfortable space with ample seating arrangements. The area was softly lit with music playing in the background, adding to the relaxed atmosphere. At the center of the gathering were tables or workspaces dedicated to the task of trimming weed, where freshly harvested cannabis buds were carefully manicured to prepare them for drying and curing. Most everyone was equipped with trimming scissors, working on buds, some as large as a beer can, removing excess leaves and quietly shaping them for market. Several bottles of wine were open, emphasizing enjoyment and companionship rather than excess. No one was smoking the crop.

Robin and her sister jumped up to greet us after our long journey. Robin embraced me with a warm hug as I introduced Randy to the group. Grinning and holding up a particularly large bud, she said, "Check this one out, Randy. It's almost as big as my hand." Impressed, Randy exclaimed, "Wow, that's a monster! This year's crop truly outdid itself." She responded, "Definitely did. I think the new organic nutrient solution we used this year made a huge difference. Plus, all that extra sunshine didn't hurt." As I took my eyes off the large bud, I said, "For sure. And it's great you're thinking about sustainability. We've got to take care of the planet if we want it to take care of us." Robin replied, "Absolutely. Speaking of taking care, how are you doing my friend? Last time we talked, you were still going through a rough patch with your wife." Looking at her, I said, "Yeah, it's been rough. It's just one of those things that still hurts, you know? Sometimes, I think it's all over and I'm getting better; then I am flooded with the pain of it all. But it's nice to be here. This is just what the doctor ordered."

Robin replied, "I hear you. Life throws curveballs, but it's how we catch them that counts. If you ever need anything, you let us know." I smiled, "Thanks, Robin. It means a lot. It's good to have friends like you and Doug around, especially at times like these. "Robin raised her voice and glass of wine, saying, "Of course, Dennis. That's what friends are for. A little trimming therapy over the next few days and a case of assorted Napa Valley reds that my sister brought up might do you some good. And hey, let's make sure we set aside some of this monster bud for later tonight after we complete this batch." "You read my mind," I said with some excitement, a little reward for a long day. "Plus, it'll be a nice way to relax and reflect on the good we're doing, both for the earth and for each other." Doug chimed in, raising his glass of wine, "Here's to your arrival, to good weed, and making the world a little greener. Now, let's get back to it. These buds won't trim themselves."

Everyone laughed, returning their focus to trimming. I looked around at the incredible scene before me and caught a smile from Robin's sister. The pungent aroma of the crop permeated the air, as several large freshly harvested plants from yesterday dangled from the rafters above me, drying by the shelter of the warm barn. Shotguns leaned against the wall near the front door, and a holstered pistol hung near a bedpost, serving as reminders of the risks we had willingly embraced.

After we settled in and finished our wine, Doug led us to his nearby camp, a ten by twelve make-shift metal shed tucked away near a small ridge and hidden by numerous trees. We engaged in light-hearted banter, testing Randy's trustworthiness with a few lines of cocaine. I had vouched for my childhood friend, easing Doug's concerns, but I think this test from Doug was something he needed to do. Returning to the large drying shed, we discovered two shabby beds adorned with marijuana remnants—a slightly more comfortable option than the wooden floor of the barn. I slept soundly that evening after a long day of travel.

The following morning, Randy and I found ourselves in awe as we ventured into the local town of Petrolia with Robin, in search of a list of supplies. Instead of rows of bread lining the small grocery store shelves, we were met with a multitude of Ziploc plastic baggies in varying sizes. Hundreds of boxes stacked neatly on the shelves. While a typical sandwich bag could hold around twenty-eight grams of the herb, the locally grown cannabis commanded higher prices than its imported counterparts and was usually sold in smaller quantities, making it appear more affordable.

Our days on this beautiful ridge were filled with a flurry of activity as we processed the dried weed. Armed with trimming scissors, we separated the buds, accumulating sticky resin on our fingers. By midday, the effects of the potent resin would penetrate through the layers of our epidermis, buzzing us without even taking a single puff. The discarded trimmings filled large dark green garbage bags, while the valuable buds were carefully arranged on the central bench for Robin's brother-in-law's inspection. He was mister quality control. Although, Doug orchestrated the entire operation. He handpicked the next batch of dried plants for processing and ensured proper ventilation during the seven to ten-day drying period.

This family-run marijuana enterprise had been nurtured by Robin and Doug's family, including her mother, over the past few years. The group invested their money, planning, and tremendous physical effort into the operation. It was a serious and high-risk business, and this was their fourth season on the same land. Chatter over the CB radio from the neighbors to the west indicated the authorities might be planning a raid soon. The sense of danger increased dramatically.

Into the Green Unknown

The land was technically overseen by the Bureau of Land Management (BLM), amidst a small group of other marijuana growers, knit together by a common goal. Congress tasked the BLM, as part of the Department of the Interior, with overseeing public lands for a variety of uses, such as energy development, livestock grazing, recreation, and timber harvesting. I don't think they had planned on its use for cultivating marijuana. Apparently the land and climate were perfect for growing this type of crop.

Humboldt County's redwoods, untamed rugged coastline, and abundant forests had fostered a relatively new tradition of cannabis cultivation. However, the 1980s marked the onset of the "War on Drugs" in Washington, with the federal government intensifying its crackdown on marijuana cultivation, particularly on public lands such as those overseen by the BLM.

The CAMP (Campaign Against Marijuana Planting) task force, spearheaded by local, state, and federal agencies, was planning an assault on marijuana growers in northern California that fall. The scale of their operation was staggering, involving over two hundred military troops, National Guardsmen, local law enforcement personnel, and federal agents. Their tactics ranged from massive eradication programs, utilizing helicopters and surveillance planes to search mountainous regions and canyons, to establishing roadblocks, conducting interrogations, and making arrests. CAMP aimed to reduce the supply of marijuana on the streets and educate the public on the perils of drug use.[1]

In a heart-pounding turn of events, we found ourselves caught in the eye of the storm during our fourth day of the harvest. Speculation ran rampant over the crackling CB radios of all the growers in the area, as rumors of an imminent raid echoed through the airwaves. A small two-passenger surveillance plane circled relentlessly above the valley that day, heightening everyone's paranoia. The scene was a whirlwind of controlled chaos, reminiscent of a Mobile Army Surgical Hospital (MASH) unit under attack. We switched to a defensive course of action. In Doug's camp, each person played their role, dismantling our "MASH unit," which had

---

1. Beecham, *CAMP Final Report*, 5–6.

made the operation work smoothly and effectively. We strongly debated leaving.

The conspicuous presence of the large drying barn, jutting out like a sore thumb against the landscape, had likely caught the attention of the survey plane flying a thousand feet above. On the last day at camp, after a lengthy group meeting, a unanimous decision was made to abandon the camp and the drying barn. We were "bugging out," a term borrowed from a real MASH unit that required the medical staff to disassemble the mobile military hospital, load it onto vehicles, and depart on a six-hour notice. We did it in just under four hours. Although, we did leave the drying barn behind.

It seemed the authorities would descend upon us soon, ready to seize plants, make arrests, and detain anyone involved. Tasked with determination, Randy, Doug, and I scurried across the sprawling fifteen-acre growing area. Armed with machetes, we identified and swiftly felled small clusters of marijuana plants—some as tall as a small ranch house, dragging them back toward the shed. It was hard to believe how big some of these plants had grown. Our objective was twofold: secure as much of the precious product as possible before our escape and establish hiding spots for the remainder. Scaling harsh terrain with determination, the three of us toiled until dusk, stashing what we could in a long double horse trailer owned by Robin's sister and brother-in-law. They had planned to head south to San Luis Obispo, where they lived. After gathering everything we needed within the limited time frame, the three vehicles set out on their pre-determined routes—all in opposite directions. The plan was to scatter and hope to reduce the likelihood of any of us being detained. Fear gripped both Randy and me. We were new to this.

Yet, uncertainty continued to gnaw, as we drove slowly north on the dirt road. It was growing dark. Had the authorities already set up checkpoints? This was not what we signed up for. Seeking refuge, we headed toward our assigned route north and spent the night at a run-down motel just off California Route 299, strategically parking the light brown truck away from prying eyes, within a heavily wooded area toward the back of the motel, while Randy nervously checked us in.

Glancing up from his newspaper, the motel clerk greeted Randy, "Evening. You need a room?" Forcing a smile, Randy looked up, "Yeah, just passing through. Need a place to crash before a long drive tomorrow." Eyeing his new customer suspiciously, he looked through the register. "We've only got two rooms available. Just the one night?" He stated, as he continued to process his new customer. His eyes flicked back and forth. "Not many folks out this way tonight." The clerk went on talking. Randy remained silent. "Your room is around back, number twelve. Here's the key. The front desk is open all night if you need anything like cigarettes, snacks or something to drink from the vending machines. Stay safe out there."

Randy was not happy he had to show his driver's license. Maybe it was a good thing he was from Colorado. Though the rural area did not have much traffic, we remained extremely cautious once inside the small musty smelling room, immediately showering away any lingering scent or evidence before attempting to sleep. I remained restless lying on the lumpy bed. Sleep was elusive.

The following day's escape plan entailed a nerve-wracking five-hour drive, beginning early in the morning toward Redding, then heading southward where we hoped to avoid encounters with law enforcement at any checkpoints set up along Interstate 5. We were two "trimmers,"—one from Colorado and the other from San Francisco, who had knowingly ventured deep into treacherous waters, far beyond our comfort zone. We were in way over our heads. A palpable sense of concern enveloped us, especially during the first hour of our drive.

Against all odds, we miraculously made it back to my apartment. Once inside, we felt safe. There were no checkpoints along our route. Astonishingly, the entire group managed to elude the impending BLM raid, which unfolded the very next day adjacent to the land we had abandoned, including the forsaken drying barn.

An article in the The Christian Science Monitor later that week confirmed the extent of the raid, reporting that:

> "Current effort in northern California is part of the major new anti-marijuana effort announced Sept. 30 by the Reagan administration. That drive reportedly will utilize military helicopters and special state-federal strike forces, augmented by National Guard troops, against those who produce a US marijuana crop estimated as worth from $10 billion to $15 billion a year. Although he says that as much as ten-thousand pounds of marijuana have been seized by armed, machete-wielding agents, Jerry Smith, director of the California bureau's San Francisco office, admits that the effort will only "scratch the surface." He points out that most marijuana plantations contain one-hundred or fewer individual plants and thus are difficult to find.[2]

It was a sobering realization that our intended escape route through Redding, would become the central headquarters of the CAMP task force the very next year. Randy and I were fortunate. Our escape was an adrenaline-fueled rollercoaster of emotions. Initially, there was an overwhelming surge of fear and panic as the realization hit us that the authorities might be closing in quickly, and the consequences of getting caught were a possibility. Every nerve was on edge as we scrambled to enact our escape plan, knowing that a misstep could lead to arrest. As we successfully evaded the task force and quietly slipped away, there was a mixture of relief and disbelief, a sense of triumph in out-smarting the law, but also the haunting awareness that danger was close and very real. The thrill of our well-planned clever escape lingered like a bittersweet victory.

Randy hastily returned to Colorado. Looking back, the reality of what I was involved in hit me hard. We had intended to produce a huge quantity of marijuana that would likely end up on the streets of San Francisco, Sacramento and Los Angeles. How many young people would this have affected? The magnitude was staggering. I was beginning to question my involvement. Is this what I really wanted to do? I think I was still wandering in the wilderness, but now I was starting to get a glimpse of where I was. Still lost.

2. Lindsay, *California Agents Attack Marijuana*, 1–2.

As thrilling as it was to escape the authorities, there was a wake-up call heard in my head. I began to question many of my self-centered motives and especially the decision to move up to Humboldt County the next year. I continued to re-evaluate my sense of purpose in life. Presently, each day involved work at the hospital, cashing my paycheck, paying my bills, and then trying to perfect the art of partying. Financially, I stayed afloat, even after absorbing most of the extra debt Bonnie and I created. There had to be more to life than this. I began to realize I was restless and in turn was searching for happiness, attempting to fill the void.

7

Seeds of Change
1982

BEFORE MY RECENT TRIP with Randy up north for the harvest, I had committed to Robin and Doug for the next growing season. Mark was my new roommate, who was Jeff's good friend from Delaware. Together we planned to pay the ten-thousand dollar buy-in to help Robin and Doug with their initial start-up costs and seed money.

We agreed to be on-site in Humboldt County from planting season to harvest. The idea of camping from March to October, tending the crop, shooing away deer, and overseeing the land appealed to me. Though I wasn't sure about the necessity of being armed, it seemed like the norm in the region, reminiscent of the wild west. Most people carried a gun. The gun-carrying folks were a mix: some could send chills down your spine, but others were genuine and would readily stretch out a helping hand without thinking twice.

For Mark, this adventure was exhilarating. He would provide the money from an insurance settlement he was owed after sustaining a serious injury earlier in the year. While working, he had fallen two stories on a construction site, landing on wooden scaffolding—probably saving his life. The fall severely damaged his left shoulder, wrist, and elbow. I used to joke that he had enough pins and screws in his body to set off any airport metal detector. After weeks of physical therapy, he moped around more easily. Waiting on Mark those first few weeks, I honed my nursing skills.

Mark had a knack for getting what he wanted; he was both persistent and clever, capable of talking the shirt off a homeless man. After Jeff's passing, I agreed he could move in temporarily until he found a place of his own. Jeff, who had tragically died in a motorcycle accident less than a mile from where we lived, had introduced Mark and me. Both he and Jeff had experimented together, smoking pot while growing up in Delaware.

Needing help with finances, this new arrangement allowed Mark to stay close to his six-year-old son after his recent separation. He had been couch hopping, as he could no longer work due to his injury, and was receiving a small amount of workers' compensation to cover rent, groceries, and his favorite party supplies like weed and whiskey. Given the circumstances of his injury, with most of his expenses covered by insurance, it left him ample time for his indulgences, including women, weed, and a white powdered drug he called "Crank." It's the street name for methamphetamine or meth. I tried it, but the nasty bitterness and the powerful stimulant weren't for me. Mark, however, enjoyed it regularly. It would keep him up for all hours, and then he would sleep a good part of the next day away. Sometimes, he would be waking up when I arrived home from work. This pattern became concerning.

Our agreement with Robin and Doug was to guard their cannabis farm during the warm growing season. If all went well, our return on investment could be substantial, possibly up to ten times our initial investment, split between us. In preparation, I purchased enough high-end camping equipment for both of us. Charging the gear to my credit card, I would worry about paying that bill later. This added to my mounting debt. The only credit card I had was nearly maxed out after purchasing our supplies.

My job at the hospital had granted my bold request for a six-month leave of absence, beginning in March, probably believing it was needed to cope with my marriage issues and the emotional stress I was experiencing. Some people in the radiation therapy department were undoubtedly aware that my breakup involved my brother. My four-wheel-drive truck would adapt well during my leave of absence in the rough country, equipped with a heavy-duty roll bar, bright trail lights and oversized tires. We were getting ready.

Over the next few months, our living quarters became a constant party hub, thanks to Mark. Our camaraderie was strained as he idled away his days and hosted late-night parties, despite knowing I had to be up early for work. I became even more frustrated when he invited his younger brother to stay "for just a little while" with us once he arrived from Delaware. He ended up staying for several weeks—those weeks turned into months, neither of them working or cleaning up after themselves.

I empathized for them and their loss of a close friend. We were all feeling the effect of losing Jeff. The night he died, a full moon hung in the sky. Each month, as I gazed up at the full moon night sky, I was reminded of life's fleeting nature. He had become a good friend, always making an effort to listen, understand, and be there for me. He seemed to ask the right questions at the right time. His emotional support during my painful separation was a source of encouragement. I like to think we created some lasting memories by sharing crazy experiences and adventures together, like playing pool each week, attending concerts, and, above all, the now-famous San Francisco 49ers game. Everyone continued to speak about Dwight Clark, soaring high in the end zone as the game clock ticked down and miraculously snagged quarterback Joe Montana's six-yard pass for a victory over Dallas.

My interests and priorities shifted dramatically and I found myself increasingly questioning where I was going in life. People are often drawn to things beyond the routine. Mine was becoming God. The harrowing experience and near escape from the authorities in Humboldt County had left me introspective, thinking more about God's purpose and love for me. Was there a plan for me? I felt there had to be more to life than the cycle of a long work-week, cashing paychecks, partying, and then repeating it all again the following week.

We continued to party. As we rapidly approached our agreed departure date for Humboldt County, I had notified my landlord that we would be moving out on the fifteenth. Things moved faster than I expected.

With our pot-growing departure just weeks away, I made a life-altering decision during a party at Robin and Doug's, where we were celebrating the upcoming planting season. Something in me was feeling unsettled. I nervously decided to bow out of our cannabis venture, hinting at a divine calling pulling me away. Barely a week later, a drunk driver crashed into my new truck, parked on the road outside my apartment, leaving it in need of extensive repairs. A sign from above? I pondered. I was not happy reacting to the new situation. Now I had no job, no deal with Robin and Doug, and no transportation. Confusion and uncertainty became my new companions.

In the time before the digital era, communication was much slower. Letters and phone calls (with "long distance rates") were the primary means of communicating with friends and loved ones. The very next day after my truck was violently pushed up onto the sidewalk and into the car parked in front of it, I received a God-inspired letter from my born-again brother Don, penned on March 6, 1983. The timing of the letter stunned me. This is what he wrote:

> "As I was having trouble falling asleep tonight, God brought you to my mind. I began to pray for you and for the protection and love of Jesus to be in your life. I sensed the struggle and battle going on in the heavens over you. I am sure that you are a very special person in God's plan. He showed me that I could pray for you and trust in his promise even if I didn't know where you were or how to get a hold of you. I feel close to you tonight even in my absence. I know in the miracle of creation that God made my spirit so that it would be sensitive to you. I can't explain that, but know that your specialness has been revealed to me. May God richly bless you in the days to come . . . may he guide

you in your decisions and anoint your mind. Be prepared for the struggle and a fierce battle if you decide to continue to seek the way of love that Jesus has begun. He will walk with you and even carry you if necessary. Trust in him; he is reliable. I'll write again soon, just a note of love and encouragement for you."

My immediate reaction would be difficult to put into words as I re-read the note that evening. I felt a deep connection to the struggle and battle going on in the heavens over me. There was a growing awareness inside that God was out there looking for me—who recognized me—who loved me despite my past. In that moment, I believed that the God of all creation had a unique plan for me. A special plan designed just for me, despite my sinfulness, my selfishness, and my stubbornness to believe. It felt as if God was saying to me, "I see you in all your flaws and weaknesses, Dennis—but, I will still love you—nothing can separate us" (Rom 8:39).

8

Unseen Grace
1983

GROWING AND CULTIVATING MARIJUANA had become a thing of the past. Instead, I was embarking on an exciting new journey, uncertain of where it would lead. I had decided to trust this powerful, unseen force that seemed to have a grip on me—it was something I couldn't easily explain.

Fortunately, even with my truck in the body shop, I could walk to work before my planned six-month leave of absence started. However, when I asked my supervisor if I could return to work, I was not surprised to learn I couldn't. My supervisor, Amy, had already hired a therapist to cover my leave of absence. While it wasn't Amy's fault, it left me questioning what to do next.

Stepping away from the cannabis venture brought a significant amount of uncertainty. Life would be tentative for a while, but I wasn't all that nervous. I felt a newfound peace within. The next six months would provide an opportunity for inner reflection before returning to work at the hospital in the fall.

In recent months, I had begun attending church after a long break beginning in eighth grade. I particularly enjoyed hearing Father John preach at Mass. He was the same priest I spoke with while making rounds at the hospital several times a week. He was so helpful in transporting patients from the oncology floor to the therapy department. He and I had a friendly relationship. When I went to Mass, I often sat in the back of the large church, hoping no one would notice my presence. God saw me there, busy developing an unseen connection in my heart. When I did go to Mass, it was usually late on Sunday morning, giving me time to sleep in and clear my head after a night of partying.

One Sunday after the service, I talked to Father John and asked, "Does God really see me?" He was a great listener and never judged me. I always felt accepted by him, despite considering myself part of an advanced group of sinners. He placed his hand on my shoulder and paused momentarily, perhaps searching for divine guidance. "Dennis, I think we all have the desire to be seen. We all want to be validated and cherished. You're not alone in this. Whether it's the yearning for your mother's gaze or the desire to be accepted among friends—at our core we all truly want to be seen and understood. Although, the depths of our heart's desires can only be quenched when we embrace Jesus Christ. It is in his love, understanding, and acknowledgment that we find solace. He sees us right where we are, understands us, and the circumstances we find ourselves in." He had my attention. I was listening intently.

Father John expanded on his response that day by sharing a story from the New Testament. "Dennis, do you remember the account from the Gospel where Jesus interacts with the Samaritan woman at the well (John 4:4–26)? We read it at Mass last week. It's remarkable that the woman would speak with Jesus, a Jew, or even engage in conversation with him, given the deep-rooted animosity between Jews and Samaritans at the time. They didn't like each other at all. Furthermore, cultural norms would have frowned upon a man speaking to a woman alone in such a setting, especially by an isolated well some distance from town. The customary time for women to fetch water was earlier in the day when it was cooler. The fact that she was there, alone in the heat of the day, suggested something was wrong. Perhaps she was alienated from her community. She wasn't comfortable going in the morning."

He paused for a bit, then continued, "Yet, in this encounter with the women at the well, we see God's capacity to understand her situation and offer her living water. As he spoke with her, Jesus addressed her complex past: her previous five husbands and the man she was living with now was not her husband. She was astonished that he knew all this about her. How could this be? Despite her status as a societal outcast and her personal transgressions, Jesus neither shuns her nor condemns her. Instead, he offers her a path to spiritual awakening. He sees her right where she is—and loves her unconditionally. I think God is just like that with us. He sees us right where we are, even in our pain."

The story reminded me that God probably sees me as well. His grace meets me on my own ragged road. My comfort lies in knowing that God wants a personal relationship with me. God's love is so encompassing that he took human form in Jesus Christ to be among us. Jesus doesn't stand distant from our afflictions; he understands our vulnerabilities, our weaknesses and extends compassion and grace exactly where we need it and when we need it. The story triggered something deep within me. I realized, I too was at the well, thirsty—looking for some of that living water.

I needed some of that grace he extended to the women at the well. I had accumulated plenty of troubles and afflictions. The list was long. My truck repairs were taking much longer than expected. I had nowhere to live; this week, staying with friends in Oakland. My steady source of income was soon to dry up. My savings were evaporating. I continued to drift from one friend's couch to another after moving out of my apartment.

Amidst this chaos, a friend generously offered her garage for storage and care for my cat, while I tried to figure out my next move. Needing a respite from the turmoil, I decided to arrange a two-week visit to my parents in Barrington, yearning to see them and express my gratitude. However, I didn't have enough money to buy a plane ticket. I would attempt to charge it to my credit card and worry about paying the bill later. I really wanted to visit my family.

Remarkably, my credit card, which had been reported lost and had several other complications, allowed me to book a round-trip flight from San Francisco to Boston on United Airlines. Against all odds, the transaction was approved. On top of that, I wasn't sure how much room I had left on my credit limit. I was making the minimum payments each month and it wasn't going away very quickly.

Was the airline ticket another nudge from the divine? I couldn't help but wonder. At the moment, it didn't matter. I was thrilled to have made the arrangements. Something felt different, but I couldn't put my finger on it. I truly wanted to see my parents and tell them how much I loved them. This new connection with God was transforming me.

After landing in Boston, I took the fifty-minute bus ride to Providence and then a second one to Barrington, feeling a surge of emotions and memories washing over me. I remembered the nostalgic walk across the Barrington river bridge to my parents' house. This was the well-worn path I followed for years; a fifteen-minute walk to and from high school. The bus stop from Providence is directly across the street from the high school and bridge. It was a cool day, and the breeze picked up and felt colder as I slowly walked across the bridge, gazing downriver. The tide was low, exposing the mud and broken shells near the water's edge. The stale smell of low tide and invigorating salt air brought back vivid memories of jumping off the bridge to cool off during the hot summer days of my youth.

The familiar smell of the house and the sound of their welcoming echoing from the kitchen all brought back a rush of memories. We exchanged warm hugs. Later that evening, I sat down with my mom and dad and looked into their eyes—those same eyes that had nurtured and guided me all these years. "Mom, dad," I began, my voice a little shaky yet sincere, "I wanted to tell you how deeply I appreciate you both. All the sacrifices you've made, the lessons you've taught me, and the unconditional love you've showered upon me. I may not say it often enough, but please know that every day I'm more and more grateful for the two of you." The room fell into a heavy silence, punctuated only by the sound of sniffles, a reminder that sometimes words can hardly convey the depth of emotions felt in one's heart. Jesus was metaphorically calling me home. My mother and father had loved me unconditionally over all those years, despite my reckless choices.

It reminded me of what the father of the prodigal son might have said when he welcomed his lost son home. In the story, the father is overwhelmed with joy and excitement at his son's return and holds a big feast in his honor, saying, "For this my son was dead, and is alive again; he was lost, and is found. And they began to celebrate" (Luke 15:18–27). I was home.

During my east coast visit, I spent most of my time with my parents. We actually did things together. I enjoyed being around them, spending little time with my pot-smoking friends still living in Barrington. Instead, my parents and I engaged in some much-needed yard work, took long walks down to one-hundred-acre cove, and occasionally went out to lunch together.

We also planned a drive up to Maine to spend time visiting Don, Jan and their new addition to the family. My parents were especially excited to see their grandchildren, including new ones that had just arrived earlier that year. Two I had not met. On the way, we stopped in Massachusetts to visit my twin brother and his family. He had added another grandchild to my parents' list that year—my brother's first. My visit to New England was a terrific opportunity to reconnect. It was very special.

During this trip, I also learned that two hospitals in Maine were actively searching for a radiation therapist. At that time, there were only two radiation therapy programs in New England—one in Vermont and the one I attended in Boston—making it difficult for Maine hospitals to recruit and retain radiation therapists.

Uncertain about whether I would remain in California, I applied for both jobs as part of a newly devised backup plan. I remember telling my parents to wait in the car when we arrived at Maine Medical Center in Portland. I thought it would only take a few minutes to fill out the application, but nearly an hour later, I returned to the parking lot, apologizing for the delay.

The medical staff had not seen a radiation therapist looking for a job for quite a while and were excited to hear my story, asking me all kinds of questions, including why I might be moving to Maine. I told several of the doctors I wasn't sure what I was going to do, but I had a good vibe about what they were doing in this part of New England.

Not long after returning to California, I made the decision to take the Maine Medical Center job. I felt God was calling, gently leading me to a better place. Although it would be about ten-thousand dollars less in annual salary (equal to about thirty-thousand dollars today), I felt it was a good choice. My brother and sister-in-law, living in New Gloucester, offered to let me stay at their house until I found an apartment of my own. I was leaving sunny California, transitioning from the fast lane to the slow lane. Life in Maine would surely move at a much slower pace. I had about a month to wrap things up in California; pack things up from storage, get my cat, and drive back to Maine.

Earning money was not the same motivator it had once been. I was now searching for a different kind of treasure. I was reminded of a bible verse, "Do not lay up for yourselves treasures on earth, where moth and rust destroy and where thieves break in and steal, but lay up for yourselves treasures in heaven, where neither moth nor rust destroys and where thieves do not break in and steal. For where your treasure is, there your heart will be also (Matt 6:19–21). I was finding it hard to believe that accumulating wealth did not have the power over me it once had. It was freeing. In contrast, the drive to earn money was deeply rooted from an early age—selling golf balls, digging clams and delivering the Providence Journal. I believed that hard work, sacrifices, and the accumulation of wealth was a means to achieve success and a higher standard of living. Was I truly making the right decision?

9

A New Dawn
1983

As I prepared myself for the journey to Utah Lake Campground, just outside Salt Lake City, my heart was filled with uncertainty and excitement. Departing California brought with it a sense of anticipation. Camping under the star-studded night sky promised to be enjoyable. It was the call of the unknown that fueled my spirit that day—that touched me deeply. My cat had provided me unconditional love throughout these many months of marriage troubles. He was not traveling well that first day, cowering on the floor partly under the seat. AC seemed a bit apprehensive, but stayed close during our pit stops, perhaps sensing the excitement that lay ahead. Well, he couldn't go too far—he was in a harness attached to a leash.

Approaching the halfway point to Colorado, it was getting dark, so I pulled off-road in my newly repaired truck and made my way to a quiet desert area of Utah under some trees where we would spend our second night together. Exposed to the stars that night, AC crawled down into the sleeping bag again, keeping my feet warm. It was nice. Although, sleep was restless and morning came early along with an unexpected dew covering everything.

Our journey took us through the picturesque mountainous terrain of Nevada and Utah, all at an average elevation about five-thousand feet. Both states are among the highest in the United States in terms of average elevation. Our next stop was Randy's, nestled between Denver and Boulder. I had made this same journey at least a half dozen times, especially during my six month leave of absence from the hospital. They welcomed me each time, helping me make sense of the transformation going on inside of me.

Our extended pit-stop began with a warm embrace from Randy and Cathy. She was pregnant with their first child, carrying the baby compactly and not having gained too much weight. Her complexion radiated her joy. They were both happy to see me and open their home for several days. I parked my over-packed pickup truck and U-Haul trailer along the side of their condo where I would not have to back it up when leaving. I was still learning how to back up a trailer on the first or second try.

Randy and I shared a lifelong bond that began on the playground of our elementary school and continued through our most recent journey to Humboldt County. Together, we had learned to swim, dared each other to explore the predictable effects of beer and weed during our early high school years, and then ventured out together to the University of Rhode Island, where we mastered the art of partying—academics took a back seat. Neither of us graduated, and our paths gradually diverged as we navigated the unpredictable twists and turns of life.

During my time at the university, I switched majors several times before gravitating toward a health education degree. It was exciting to be in classes with young women, mostly nursing majors, who had a clear sense of purpose. I was one of only two guys taking the anatomy and physiology class. Much of what we studied, including the tiny cells under the microscope and the hundreds of bones of the human body triggered a deep curiosity within me that semester—something I couldn't fully explain or begin to understand. The seeds of fascination with the details of the human body had been planted in me. They were quietly growing, taking root. Randy and I enjoyed each other's company for a couple of days

A New Dawn

before I left, just hanging out and connecting. We did some intense hiking near Boulder and slept under the stars.

Our three-day stay evaporated quickly and AC and I hit the road again. We would embark on the next leg of our adventure, heading south to Albuquerque on US Route 25. The indirect path to Maine included several days of driving through the southern expanse of the country, complete with planned stops to visit Bonnie in Georgia and Jeff's parents in Delaware.

Amarillo Texas and Oklahoma City was uncharted territory. As we ventured southward, the terrain gradually transformed, revealing an expanse of rolling fields, punctuated by the occasional small town and roadside diners. The highways were like lifelines connecting small towns in all directions, stretching endlessly through the open skies and horizon, offering a sense of both solitude and connection to the vastness of the southern Midwest. It was an enchanting drive leaving the mountains of Colorado—more desert-like, dry and barren. This mirrored my feelings inside.

We stopped for the night after driving about ten-hours, pitched the small tent I had purchased for just this purpose and enjoyed the fire, drifting deep in thought. My cat was not interested in the fire and opted to sleep in the truck. Sitting by the fire that night brought a peace I hadn't experienced in some time. As I gazed into the orange glow, I found myself naturally quieting, becoming more attuned to my inner self and the present moment. This stillness helped me examine my emotions, and gain insights into my never-ending search for happiness. In this serene communion with fire's basic dance, I found both a needed escape from the bustling chaos of life and a unique new connection to the unseen God. As the flames flickered and swayed, casting their warm glow upon me, I could not help but feel drawn into the flame's mysterious movement that seemed to speak to the deepest part of my spirit. I became more aware of the gradual but powerful changes stirring deep inside. My spirit had been restless for so many years, and now was finding rest in God. Peace seeped into me that night.

Thomas Merton comments on the pursuit of happiness in his autobiography of faith in *Seven Story Mountain*, "If what most people take for granted were really true—if all you needed to be happy was to grab everything and see everything and investigate every experience and then talk about it, I would have been a very happy person, a spiritual millionaire. If happiness were merely a matter of natural gifts, I would never have entered a Trappist Monastery when I came of age."[1]

Traveling along US Route 40 was the most convenient and quickest way to make it to Georgia, where Bonnie was now living. We had planned to meet as I passed through that part of the country and talk. It brought me through cities and landscapes I had never traveled to before. The Texas panhandle offered the wide-open spaces and flat plains characteristic of the southwest. We stopped for the night to visit the Palo Duro Canyon State Park, the second-largest canyon in the United States. Our campsite overlooked parts of the ragged terrain and rusty red dirt common to the area. It was very dry and hot. AC chose to sleep in the truck again.

Our planned rendezvous took place just north of Atlanta, along US Route 85. We met for lunch at Rosati's Pizza and talked about what had happened over the last year. She was aware I had taken a new position at Maine Medical Center and would stay with my brother Don's family for a while. Wayne and her had broken it off after about a year of living together in Providence. Her mother knew some people in Georgia who were involved in the fashion industry where she could re-group and sort things out.

As we walked together after lunch, the warm Georgia air carried whispers of the past. The memories of happier times lingered along the path. We reached a vast clearing overlooking a quiet deserted lake. Bonnie and I sat on a fallen log together, the silence between us no longer uncomfortable but filled with a shared understanding. I took out a small photo of us, one where we were younger—laughing, carefree and full of life.

"I am not sure what will become of us Dennis," Bonnie said, her voice still tinged with sadness but stronger than before. I nodded, taking a deep breath. "I'm not sure either. I do know we both have experienced a lot of pain." Bonnie added, "I'm so sorry for

---

1. Merton, *Seven Story Mountain*, 20.

everything and hope you can forgive me. I will always remember your thoughtfulness and the way you could make me smile. You'll always have a place in my heart."

We sat there for a while, the silence now a comforting embrace. As the sun began to grow lower, casting a tinted glow over the landscape, I felt a sense of peace between us. It was a moment of quiet reflection. Bonnie reached for my hand, and I squeezed it gently. "Thank you for meeting me here before you head to Maine." We stood up, ready to leave but not to forget. The drive north felt introspective.

Arriving in New England, crossing over the New York state line, felt like a victory, after so many days on the road and so many cities behind me. Surprisingly, driving long distances takes its toll both physically and emotionally. I was tired. Navigating Connecticut was something I had done many times before—always a challenge. Western Rhode Island was next, a region of captivating contrasts, where the quaint charm of historic villages meets the energy of downtown Providence, passed quickly and brought back memories. After all, Rhode Island is the smallest of all the states. Driving from one side to the other takes less than an hour.

Driving down the winding road, locally known as the Wampanoag Trail into Barrington was a nostalgic experience, especially as the river came into view just beyond the vast expanse of one-hundred-acre-cove. It always brought back memories of my youth. The strong winds out of the south created whitecaps on the river that day. It reminded me of my early days of growing up on the cove with my twin. We would try, unsuccessfully, to row our eight-foot pram against the wind—a tiring and exhausting effort—much like my three-thousand-mile drive from California.

I thought of the boat as a metaphor for my life. Rowing a boat against the wind is possible, but one becomes frustrated and tires quickly. It mirrored my own life up to this point along my journey. My entire past moved against the wind. Now, with my spirit aligning with God's plan instead of my own, I felt I was moving with the wind, not against it, with less effort and more peace. Although, my future would still contain strong winds and powerful storms.

Looking back, I couldn't help but wonder if I had missed important clues about Bonnie's growing relationship with Wayne. They had commuted together for years while they both worked in Providence. To me, it seemed more like a convenience. I often wondered if they were more than friends, growing closer while I was in Boston. Additionally, Wayne was quick to visit California shortly after we first arrived, before she started working. In fact, he was our first visitor. Perhaps at the time, the two of them were putting the finishing touches on their plan.

As time passed, I remained open to the possibility of reconciliation with Bonnie, determined to honor God's plan for marriage, and patience became a guiding virtue. I met with people at my new church and several ministers at other churches in the area to seek guidance. No one had a good answer to my problem. Most didn't know what to say. I was trying to do the right thing, but I found no good counsel.

Don and his family had decided to move to Brunswick, seeking closer ties to their church community. Several living opportunities presented themselves that spring, and I faced a difficult choice regarding which arrangements would work best. I could follow them to the Brunswick area or find an apartment in Portland, drawing me closer to work and the friendships I had there. Portland, with its colorful coastal scenery, was inviting.

Alternatively, I could move in with a friend in New Gloucester. Here, the embrace of familiarity with my church friends would surround me like a warm, comforting blanket. For months, I sought input from anyone who would lend an ear, exploring my options in all three areas. My brother and his family had graciously accommodated me since arriving, but it was time to find a place of my own. Little did I know, as I was praying for guidance, that the answer to my living situation would manifest in the most extraordinary manner.

I traveled deeper along my new spiritual path, balancing it with work and pleasure. I was working about forty-five hours a week, attending Bible study, and hiking with friends on weekends. Each morning, I devoted time to prayer, though I wasn't always successful. In the past, I was never very good at listening to God or anyone for that matter. Especially growing up; I was stubborn and selfish. Just ask my twin brother David. He would likely share some interesting tales of my self-centered youth. After all, he was by my side most of the time, shadowing me as we grew up together. I later realized, he tolerated me too—he loved me unconditionally, just the way I was.

10

Solar Eclipse
1984

TOWARD THE END OF May, an unexplainable desire to pray more intensely, seeking divine direction regarding where to move, enveloped me. For days, I couldn't shake it. It persisted. I had developed a fairly consistent habit of praying each morning, sometimes studying the scriptures, praying for loved ones, or seeking guidance. I prayed humbly and openly for direction, trusting that God had a plan. My prayer life was developing consistency. It was like I was learning a new language, and the more I practiced it, the more progress I made.

Learning a new language is akin to opening a window to a world filled with unique experiences and unexpected pleasures. The learning process required patience, dedication, and an open mind. It began with mastering the basics—simple phrases and vocabulary. As I progressed, I began to grasp the rhythm and flow of the new language, gradually feeling more comfortable and confident in my ability to communicate more effectively. Practice each day was important.

When it came to learning to pray in a new language, the experience became deeply personal. I learned that prayer was an intimate conversation with God, and conveying our innermost thoughts and feelings is daunting at first. It requires both sharing and listening. More listening. As I became more familiar with the process, my prayer evolved from rote recitation to genuine expressions of thoughts and faith. This not only deepened my understanding of the new language but also enriched my spiritual life.

During prayer that day, I heard a voice, clear and distinct. It was a type of vision, I think. I was instructed to go outside at noon the next day and look to the sky, assuring me that a circular sign would guide my way. Really? The message initially bewildered me, filling me with doubt and questions. It happened so quickly and would have been easy to dismiss. Could this truly be the Holy Spirit speaking to me? It seemed too outlandish for a new believer like me. I wrote down what I had heard in my journal and sat quietly for some time, contemplating God's nature and trying to be still. There was such peace—the more I remained still, the more intense the peace.

What kind of sign would I see in the sky? Would it be a solar halo or an intricate cloud formation? And why at noon? Yet, beneath my skepticism, a glimmer of hope and excitement ignited within me. Strangely, part of me believed that God was communicating with me and that the following day would reveal something very special. Despite the forecast predicting light rain and clouds, I embraced this puzzling message. When I arrived at the hospital that morning, there was no sun to be seen anywhere, only thick clouds which had rolled into the port of Portland overnight. Now, how was I going to see anything in the sky?

After the morning treatment schedule, which ran late due to unforeseen patient issues, we could all re-fuel over our one-hour lunch break. Most of the therapists, nurses, and doctors remained inside the hospital, especially on a cloudy, overcast day. Not me. I had plans to head toward The Vaughn Street Variety to purchase a sandwich, as was sometimes my routine. It was a short walk from the radiation therapy department entrance, which was strategically positioned two stories underground near the side of the main hospital entrance. There were no windows in our department. It was common practice to use the earth to shield the high intensity radiation from the general public—the thick earth did just that.

My pulse quickened as I walked toward the elevator. There was a distinct dryness in my mouth as I ascended the two floors. Anticipation mingled with doubt as I emerged outside under a very overcast gray sky and moved toward the variety store. I then stumbled upon a scene just outside the store's entrance that left me awestruck and bewildered.

Dr. Seitz, a physician I worked with, stood on the sidewalk outside the sandwich shop in the damp gray fog. We had a good relationship, as he was easygoing and loved the cookies that patients would sometimes bring in to show appreciation for all we were doing. We were helping them fight their battle against cancer, and they showed appreciation when bringing in all sorts of goodies and small gifts. Clad in his white lab coat, he had also purchased a sandwich. He boldly held a piece of exposed x-ray film at arm's length—an opaque, dark gray, almost black sheet about the size of a small plate between his fingers and gazed up through the clouds.

He explained that an x-ray film would shield our eyes from the harmful rays, filtering the intense brightness of the sun during this eighty-five percent total eclipse. What did he say? I wasn't sure I heard exactly what he said.

It was just after noon, and there, unfolding before my eyes, the moon was slowly moving across the sun, casting an otherworldly shadow from a circle in the sky. In fact, two circles—one for the moon, one for the sun—converged in perfect harmony before me. My heart raced with joy, like a child opening a birthday gift. I was in awe and felt a bit giddy. In that moment, an incredible amount of faith welled up within me, a mix of truth and emotion I had not known before. I felt whole and complete, like the circle.

I confided in Dr. Seitz as we exchanged the small piece of x-ray film, telling him about the vision I had regarding the eclipse the day before. I was risking it when I asked him, "What do you think about God and science and how they interact together?" Dr. Seitz handed me the piece of x-ray film, pondered for a moment, and said, "You know, throughout history, the relationship between

Solar Eclipse

God and science has proven complex and at times contentious, fueling debates and conflicts between religious and scientific communities. I was just talking to Dr. Phelps about this yesterday," proclaimed Dr. Seitz, "and he believes, as I do, that some argue that science and religion are fundamentally incompatible, representing divergent ways of viewing and understanding the world. Science, he posited, relies on empirical evidence and the scientific method, like we see in our radiation therapy journal articles, while religion hinges on faith and supernatural beliefs—two contrasting approaches."

"On the other hand," I countered, "still others contend that science and religion could coexist, offering distinct yet complementary understandings of our existence. Science, I asserted, unravels the intricacies of the natural world, while religion provides powerful insights into the meaning and purpose of human life. It's hard to believe that people don't see God in an eclipse like this today." As Dr. Seitz turned to leave, he was shaking his head, telling me, "Enjoy the rest of the eclipse, Dennis. You can keep the x-ray film. I have to go."

For some time, I had been struggling with my purpose in life, convinced that humans have a special relationship with the divine. This connection provided me with a sense of belonging and purpose. Was I part of a divine plan or mission? Did God desire a relationship with me? How would I respond?

A day later, I found a newspaper article describing the eclipse—a celestial event that touched millions of lives across the nation on May 31, 1984. The reporter described the eclipse in detail:

> "From Louisiana to North Carolina, people today were afforded a rare glimpse of a nearly total solar eclipse that turned noontime into an eerie twilight and briefly framed the black shadow of the moon in a spectacular necklace of light. The 'diamond necklace' effect, caused as the moon passes directly in front of the sun, was seen by millions of people who gathered in cities in the south to witness the full effect of the eclipse, the last major solar eclipse in the nation this century. Although the eclipse was most dramatic in the southeast, some sort of partial

eclipse was visible, where weather permitted, throughout all of the nation except Alaska. Rain and clouds obscured views of the eclipse along much of the east coast, including New York City. Parts of North Carolina and Virginia, which fell along the line where the moon cast its darkest shadow, also did not see the eclipse because of weather."[1]

I saw it! I was trying hard to grasp the fact that the creator of the universe had conspired to align my path with that of the eclipse. I was speechless. Later that next day, I pondered what had just happened, re-running the scenario over and over in my mind. I was filled with excitement and told the story of the moon passing in front of the sun, moving in a northeast direction to whoever would listen. In my human existence, I could not understand how I had received specific instructions in my heart the day before about seeking direction from a circle in the sky. How could a circle show me the way? How could this be, as a circle is round, complete, and whole? Lines generally provide direction, not circles. How could I have known it was going to be an eclipse, even on a cloudy day? After this amazing event unfolded, I was left humbled and very reflective. I delved into the scriptures, seeking understanding. Three verses resonated in my soul:

- "for they cried out to God in the battle, and he granted their urgent plea because they trusted in him."(1 Chr 5:20b)
- "Then you will call upon me and come and pray to me, and I will hear you." (Jer 29:12)
- "that the Lord your God may show us the way we should go, and the thing that we should do."(Jer 42:3)

These ancient words echoed throughout my being, instilling in me an incredible sense of faith and purpose. The divine circle in the sky had provided me with a tangible sign, a glimpse into the mysterious workings of God's plan. Without a doubt, I was seriously considering moving to Brunswick. This was northeast of where I was currently living, leading me to follow the path of the

---

1. Schmidt, *Millions Treated to Solar Eclipse*, 1.

eclipse, which had distinctly moved in a northeast direction that day. What awaited me?

Recognizing the value of seeking guidance, I eagerly anticipated sharing my extraordinary encounter on Vaughn Street with my prayerful brother Don, over the weekend, after they returned from a visit to Rhode Island. He and his family had made plans to relocate to the Brunswick area from New Gloucester, having sold their house. They were moving shortly.

I had the very real option to join them on their journey, drawing closer to a new church group that had experienced significant growth over the last year. They were open to sharing their home with me again. It seemed God was calling me—directing my next move.

11

Ruins to Renewal
1984

TIME WAS HEALING ME, and living with my brother and his family significantly contributed to that healing. They loved me just as I was. I felt different now, shedding some of the masks I had worn to conceal the real Dennis. The air in Maine was fresh and clean, no smog, no haze in the air. To my amazement, this is how I began to feel inside.

Every month, the prayer group in Brunswick hosted a "Dinner Club" fundraiser on Saturday nights, commencing at six o'clock. Members of the group volunteered to cook, clean, and serve a hearty four-course meal to a gathering of between one-hundred to one-hundred-fifty guests. Baked haddock was a favorite among many regulars. After the meal, many volunteers entertained the guests with skits, songs and musical performances, often inspired by biblical teachings or popular stories.

I was still living in New Gloucester when I volunteered for my first event. That evening, the theatrical production centered on the well known tale of The Wizard of Oz, where Jesus takes on the role of the wizard, guiding Dorothy and her new friends on their quest for meaning and purpose. The journey symbolized their pursuit of truth along the yellow brick road. The play, lasting about an hour with a short intermission, captivated the audience with its splendid acting and inviting message. This was my first exposure to such a faith-filled drama presentation, and it resonated deep within me. I was reminded that, I too, was on a yellow brick road searching for truth and meaning.

Volunteering at the Dinner Club, I was assigned to wait tables alongside Jeanne, a familiar face and someone I had grown to know over the past months. Jeanne had a warm, friendly demeanor. She was shorter and younger than I. Her long dark brown hair had a fullness that complemented her round face, striking blue eyes and welcoming smile. Outwardly, Jeanne moved with confidence and purpose, but inwardly, she was a bit shy and troubled.

The volunteer coordinator, aware of my novice status, paired me with this blue-eyed veteran to ensure I received proper guidance throughout the evening. Jeanne treated me with gentleness and concern; she was a good listener and was aware of what I was going through. While serving each course, we engaged our table by listening to their stories and sharing a bit about ourselves. I enjoyed getting to know some of the guests and spending time with her. This month, like many others I was told, was sold out. In fact, it was often difficult to get a reservation at the Dinner Club, especially for a large group.

Watching Jeanne's interactions with the guests at our table, observing her ease in sharing and her genuine care for others, I discovered an unexpected joy in serving together. We complemented each other, both of us easily engaging folks at our table. She made the evening fun and run smoothly.

When the event wrapped up, many of the volunteers and some lingering guests would gather by the large stone fireplace, where flames consumed the evening's wood. "So, what did you think of the performance?" I asked Jeanne as we sat by the fire. Gazing into the fire, she replied, "It was very moving. I love how they intertwined the story of the Wizard with our faith journey. It really resonated with me." "I felt the same way. It's like we're all on the yellow brick road searching," I said, holding my hands up to the fire, feeling the warmth. She nodded. "Exactly. And sometimes, the journey is as important as the destination." I paused to consider this new truth and it made sense.

Feeling a connection, I asked. "Speaking of journeys, can I ask for your input on something I've been dealing with? After experiencing that powerful solar eclipse in Portland, I'm considering moving to Brunswick." "That sounds like a great idea," Jeanne said, her face brightening. "It's a wonderful group of people, mostly our age. Have you figured out where you would live yet?" Thinking about her question, I said, "I'm still praying about that—not sure where I'd live. I think the commute to Portland from Brunswick would be about the same." Jeanne paused and looked directly into my eyes and said, "Dennis, I think it's important for you to follow God's prompting, especially since you felt it was an important answer to prayer. And it would be nice to have you closer, you make a good server." Referring to the eclipse, I asked her, "Do you think God really speaks to us that way?" She replied, "I certainly do. There are plenty of examples similar to yours in the Bible. Sounds like God is trying to get your attention."

She then shared about her father's ailing condition with me, looking somber and somewhat concerned. My work with cancer patients at the hospital gave us a reason to talk about her dad each time we met. I liked answering her questions and giving her comfort and advice about her father. He was quite sick, and the more help, the better. "I really appreciate you helping me with my dad," she said, her voice tinged with sadness. "It's been hard seeing him like this." I wasn't sure what to say after a long silence, "He seems like a strong man. I hope he gets through this." She became quiet, hiding her emotions. She had a terrible, worried look about her. Regrouping, she quickly changed the subject, asking me how I was doing. "How are you holding up with everything?" she asked, her concern evident. "Honestly, it's been a long couple of months," I admitted. "I'm still trying to figure out what to do with my marriage. Part of me hopes we can work things out, even if everyone thinks I'm crazy for trying. Another part of me wants to move on and start over." "It's not crazy to want to fix things," Jeanne said softly. "But sometimes, moving on can be the best thing for both of you—a new beginning."

On one hand, I believed that God wanted my wife and me to get back together, to work on rebuilding our troubled relationship. As my understanding of God's nature deepened, I truly forgave Bonnie for her infidelity, wiping the slate clean between us and allowing for a fresh start. Forgiveness is a gift we can offer to another. God had lovingly forgiven me, absolving me of all my transgressions—wiped my slate clean. This was the reason I was in Maine. My failed marriage had been a good teacher.

She lived in Georgia while I lived in Maine, making the prospect of meeting halfway a daunting challenge. My mind conjured up images of hiking the Appalachian Trail, which spans from Georgia to Maine. If we both embarked on the trail, journeying toward each other until we converged at the halfway point near Harpers Ferry, West Virginia, it might symbolize reconciliation. However, we both hesitated to leave the comfort and security of our new locations. Thus, we remained apart, not interested in hiking with each other.

Later that fall, after several more Dinner Club events, I found myself working on a construction project at Jeanne's house. She shared the house with four friends. The two bedrooms and living area on the lower level remained unfinished. As a result, the five roommates shared two bedrooms and a single bathroom on the upper floor.

They pooled their resources and made every effort to make it work. Jeanne's selflessness was evident as she organized several friends who needed a place to live and share expenses. Their split-level ranch-style home, like others in the neighborhood, had staggered levels that were connected by separate staircases. Off the main level were two sets of stairs: one led to the upstairs rooms, and the other to the basement. The basement remained unfinished, with two by four walls outlining most of the rooms and nearly all of the wiring in place for electrical sockets and some overhead lighting.

Over the next several months, with the help from a few friends, I spearheaded efforts to complete the two additional bedrooms and construct a second bathroom. It was enjoyable visiting this lively group of women. The banter in the house was enjoyable, as was the first-rate food. Often, after a day's work, we would linger and talk. The longer it took to finish the project, the better it seemed to me. I believe we all felt the same way. They were so excited to gain more privacy.

On one Saturday afternoon, Jeanne and I worked together, cutting wood for a bedroom closet. We were the construction crew that day. Our conversation was mostly focused on the task at hand. I think I surprised her when she asked me how I was doing with my marriage problems. I had wanted to tell her but was uncertain how to bring it up, so I proclaimed, "Almost miraculously, Bonnie sent me a copy of the official divorce papers from Georgia. I didn't need to take any action. I didn't have to do a thing—some lawyer in Georgia had set me free. The news was a surprise, as unbeknownst to me, Bonnie and her mother had been working with her lawyers for some time to help her move forward." Jeanne gave a big hug and said, "I am so happy for you Dennis. What a relief you must feel. Wow, now you can get on with your life."

I felt a sense of liberation, a weight lifted from my shoulders. I had invested so much effort into trying to salvage this marriage, but her unwillingness to meet halfway left us wandering apart. We would continue hiking alone. She was resolute about remaining in Georgia, while I called Maine home. The Appalachian Trail metaphor felt apt; we were two hikers on different paths. At one time, we enjoyed hiking together, but now it seemed we would continue hiking life's trail separately and from different points of view. I began to wonder that day working in the basement with Jeanne if she likes to hike.

Bill, a member of the construction crew, mentioned that I could learn more about Jesus and his teachings by joining a group from our church traveling to Israel. It would be a three-week pilgrimage to Jerusalem with some hiking included. "Why not join us on our trip to the Holy Land, Dennis?" Bill said excitedly. "There are ten of us signed up so far, and most are our age. This isn't just a trip for retired folks. We're going to fly into Amman first and then cross over the Jordan River where Jesus was baptized, explore Jerusalem and some of the surrounding sites, and then finish up the trip in Egypt."

I wanted to know more about this once-in-a-life-time trip. I told him I would love to go, but I just couldn't afford it right now. He asked me how much I could afford and if I wanted, he would lend me the rest. Given my current bills, I could only afford to pay him back one-hundred dollars a month, but not until after Christmas. He agreed. This was another in the long list of unexpected events unfolding in my life. Things were becoming exciting. Even more exciting, it turned out that Jeanne liked hiking too. She had tried it before but just couldn't find the right partner.

12

Jerusalem
1984

BEFORE I LEFT FOR the Middle East, Jeanne had sent me a note of encouragement along with money to pick out a small cross for her mother, made from olive wood. Olive trees represent strength and longevity and are an important part of Israeli culture. The cross on which Jesus was crucified was made of the wood gathered from the olive trees near the Garden of Gethsemane in Jerusalem. She assured me she would pray for us each day. I felt reassured and encouraged.

After leaving New York City and stopping over in Amsterdam, we arrived just after sunset in the dry, dusty city of Ammon. Each day on this three-week pilgrimage, some of us rose early to pray together on the large balcony overlooking the ancient city, as hundreds of birds sang along with us. We were greeted by a magnificent sunrise on our first day. The city itself was built on a series of hills, providing stunning views of the urban landscape and warm desert surroundings. It was a hot, dry, almost mystical experience.

Breakfast at the hotel was fair. Strong coffee, scrambled eggs with toast was served, before traveling the four hours south to the lost city of Petra. Situated between the Red Sea and the Dead Sea and inhabited by various groups since prehistoric times, this sandstone-carved city of the Nabateans became a major caravan trading center along the Silk Road for the incense from Arabia, the silks of China, and the spices of India. It was a critical crossroads between Africa, Europe, and Asia. Its inhabitants were more than just desert nomads—they were pirates and robbers. The city of Petra is half-built, half-carved into the rock, and is surrounded by mountains peppered with secret passages and gorges extending into the mountains. An ingenious water management system allowed extensive settlement of an essentially arid area during the Nabataean (emerged in the fourth century BCE), Roman (conquest of Judea in sixty-three BCE), and Byzantine (from the fourth century CE until the seventh century CE) periods. It is one of the seven wonders of the world and largest archaeological sites set in the striking red sandstone landscape.[1] Some of the sandstone can actually be shaped and carved with your fingernail. It's that soft. I tried it.

On our drive south, we passed many Palestinian refugee camps and shepherds tending their flocks of goats and sheep in the hot dry landscape. It brought me back in time, reminding me of what life must have been like when Jesus walked, prayed, and ministered in parts of Palestine.

Petra was breathtaking. The sky was so blue that day and the sun so warm. Many of the natives in that area make their living through the tourists who come to visit the ancient ruins. We were a small group with dollars. I am sure we were very easy to spot. Arrangements were made ahead of time to travel by horseback through the small canyon, formed by an earthquake thousands of years earlier. This was going to be an exciting adventure into history.

Each of us in our group of twelve, mounted on a horse, was then slowly led by a guide who spoke no English. The horseback ride was a bit slow and controlled. Still, it was fun and a novel approach to this unique place on earth. Once we arrived, we encountered a lively group of peddlers. Many were set up under the shade of makeshift awnings, selling fresh fruit, nuts, and all kinds of souvenirs. As I moved about, taking in the sights and the smells

1. Milstein, *Petra*, 1–5.

surrounding us in this deep beautiful sandstone gorge, I came across a quiet elderly man who looked poor and disheveled, sitting on some flat rocks in the shade. He was selling a small collection of trinkets, stones, and old coins. We gestured back and forth on the price for a coin that caught my eye, a small one with rounded edges about the size of a dime, but thicker. It appeared to be made of bronze or some dark metal, with an image of a king on one side and an intricate design on the reverse. Later, I discovered it was a coin from the Nabataean Kingdom at a time when King Aretas IV ruled from roughly nine BC to forty AD. I couldn't believe my find. Interestingly, most historians indicate that Jesus was crucified during Passover week in twenty-nine AD.[2]

During my visit with the old man sitting in the shade, I was unaware what the coin represented for me—Jesus' visit to Earth. The coin, minted during that same time period would be a reminder of my transformative time spent in the Holy Land. This incredible symbolism surfaced years later and still gives me goosebumps. I even now have the treasured coin on display.

On day three of our tour of Palestine and Israel, we left Ammon and crossed the bridge over the Jordan River into Israel. With high security, it took forever. Just after we crossed the border, we met up with our Israeli tour guide in Jericho. It's important to note that there are rigorous requirements for becoming a tour guide in Israel. Shira, who had a separate degree in archaeology and also participated in a two-year program at the university where she studied various aspects of Israel's history, greeted us with enthusiasm. She spoke four languages and also had an in-depth understanding of Jewish, Islamic, and Christian cultures. I was impressed with how seriously the government shaped and governed their tourist industry, as each year Israel welcomed somewhere near four million visitors, many of whom were pilgrims. We were there on a once-in-a-lifetime journey to hopefully grow spiritually and visit the historical and cultural sites where Jesus lived and prayed over two thousand years earlier.

---

2. Almasri, *Petra-Holy City*, 67.

Jerusalem

We arrived in Tiberias, a fishing village on the Sea of Galilee, about lunchtime. St. Peter's fish was on the menu. The dish, deep-fried with the head and tail still on, represents the type of fish Peter and some of the other apostles might have caught in the lake. It was delicious and crunchy. Although the fish's eye remained fixed on me the entire time I was eating it. After a while, I didn't notice the fish looking at me.

Our next stop, traveling by boat, was Capernaum. It was a short six-mile excursion up the northwest part of the lake, also known as the Sea of Galilee. Our travels through this area certainly touched my heart deeply, as Jesus spent a great deal of his time preaching and healing in this area, moving from town to town advancing the kingdom of God.

A biblical story takes place in Capernaum, where Jesus instructs his new converts, Andrew and Simon Peter, to cast their nets into the lake after a long night of unsuccessful fishing. They reluctantly obey. Their catch is miraculously large, filling their nets to overflowing. Here, he instructs the two brothers: "Follow me, and I will make you fishers of men" (Matt 4:19). God had a plan for them to give up their lifestyle of catching fish and following Jesus. They were taught to share with a multitude of people about God's kingdom. These events on the Sea of Galilee mark the beginning of Jesus' ministry and the gathering of his disciples. And here I was, walking the very ground they walked, centuries earlier. It made what I had read in the bible come alive—it held more meaning.

At the same time, I too was searching for a new lifestyle. God had called me from a life of aimless wandering and selfishness in California to begin a new life, centered on Jesus. I felt called to share with those I would encounter on my journey about the powerful transformation occurring in my own life. It felt as though an invisible light was shining along my path, allowing me to see with my heart the great love God has for each of us.

Shira, our knowledgeable certified guide, led us through the historic aspects of Capernaum. She shared a captivating discovery about Jesus' life as we all sat around the outdoor tables in the shade, saying, "Capernaum was more than just a town for Jesus; it was his home for a significant part of his adult life." Her voice held a note of excitement as she shared the history of how Jesus started his ministry here: teaching in the local synagogue (Mark 1:21–24), choosing his first disciples (Matt 4:19), and gaining a reputation for miraculous healings (Mark 3:1–5).

Then, with a sense of excitement, she guided us to the heart of her story—the archaeological find that shed light on the dawn of Christianity. "Imagine, in this very place, several Italian archaeologists unearthed what is believed to be Peter's house, where Jesus himself stayed." We gathered closer as she described the location. "Beneath the remnants of an ancient church, they found a simple first-century dwelling. While larger than typical homes of its time, its simplicity was evident in the walls and a roof made of earth and straw." The site was ancient, weathered, but well-preserved.

Our guide's words painted a powerful picture. "What's truly remarkable," she continued, "is the transformation of this ordinary house after the first century AD. It's these types of changes, hinting that this was very likely Peter's house, and by extension, Jesus' home in Capernaum." She emphasized how, in archaeology, "it's often the small clues and findings that create the strongest connections to biblical figures and events. Although there's no conclusive evidence confirming this site as Peter's ancient house, layers of indirect evidence support its role in early Christianity and its connections to Jesus and Peter."

The significance of the discovery was further underscored by the findings within the old church built over the house on the very same site. Shira's enthusiasm was infectious as she spoke about the hundred-plus graffiti etched into the walls—phrases like: "Lord Jesus Christ help thy servant" or "Christ have mercy," in Greek, Syriac, or Hebrew. Accompanied by small crosses and even a sketch of a boat, these inscriptions serve as a testament to the building's pivotal role in the birth of Christianity.[3] We moved slowly through the site absorbing its significance. Our guide's narrative transported us back in time, allowing us to experience the

---

3. Biblical Archaeology Society Staff, *The House of Peter*, 1–2.

layers of history and growing faith that were intertwined in this ancient lake-side location. I was amazed.

This archeological site significantly shifted my understanding. I had witnessed the very place that perhaps the early church spent time loving one another, proclaiming Jesus' promise of redemption and love. This is where it all began. In a way, I felt connected to it. I owed my faith to those early Christians who lived, worked, and spread Jesus' message from this very spot on the globe. I appreciated the fact that this good news had been passed down to me from these early days, as we examined the artifacts on this incredible archaeological site.

Later in the afternoon, we found ourselves at an old church located on a grassy mountainside overlooking the lake. It was believed to be the very spot where Jesus imparted his compelling Sermon on the Mount with his powerful words, challenging us to love our enemies, forgive others, and care for the poor. Even though the Mass at this church was in French, a language somewhat familiar to me, a sense of awe was palpable, uniting us, a diverse group of people from all over the world. There were close to one-hundred, joined together in a shared experience of breaking bread together.

After a late dinner, we gathered around a large covered table by the lake in downtown Capernaum, exchanging our thoughts and reflections on the day. It was then that we met Marilyn, a young American woman from a nearby hotel, where there was a Jewish wedding reception a hundred yards from us. We witnessed the lively music, dancing, and bright lights surrounding those remaining after a long day of celebrating.

She joined us for a nightcap under the stars. I felt an inexplicable urge, a divine nudge perhaps, directing me to reach out to her. Our conversation effortlessly shifted to my spiritual journey and transformation over the past two years. Marilyn, herself searching, was eager and inquisitive, had questions about changing her own life, as I had. She wanted to know more about God's forgiveness and transforming power.

I told her I was open and receptive to that power, even if I wasn't certain where it brought me. My heart was different lately.

The hardness had been broken up much like a farmer breaks up the ground just before planting. God had planted new seeds of hope in the soft soil of my heart, confirming that I was redeemed—worthy in his eyes. We spoke until after midnight and I would like to think she left with a better understanding of God's love for her. Our talk was more than just words; it helped us learn about ourselves. We were both exploring new territory, gaining insights along the way.

As the long day neared its end, our group prepared for the next leg of our journey—a visit to the Jordan River. Marilyn would think about joining us tomorrow and consider her own baptism in the same river Jesus visited for his baptism. Or she could just come along for the ride. Many of us planned to renew our baptismal vows, answering several questions before dipping into the water:

- Do you reject Satan? And all his works? And all his empty promises?
- Do you believe in God, the Father Almighty, creator of heaven and earth?
- Do you believe in Jesus Christ, his only Son, our Lord, who was born of the Virgin Mary, was crucified, died, and was buried, rose from the dead, and is now seated at the right hand of the Father?
- Do you believe in the Holy Spirit, the holy catholic church, the communion of saints, the forgiveness of sins, the resurrection of the body, and life everlasting?[4]

We started our day with breakfast by the lake and then loaded up the van to drive south, from Sea of Galilee. It was so nice to have Marilyn join us on our journey that morning. She continued to seek answers to her questions from several of us on how Jesus could wash away our sins. There were seven of us ready to renew our baptismal vows including Marilyn, who would be baptized for the first time. All of us would be submerged into the same water that Jesus was baptized in by John the Baptist centuries earlier.

---

4. Bellini, *Do You Renounce Satan?*, 3.

JERUSALEM

My heart was full, as the spirit prepared me for my renewal. There were handrails anchored in the riverbed sloping from the shore and moving down into the water; one on your left one on your right, guiding you to where your entire body would be submerged. Here, you would make a commitment to follow Jesus and seek his guidance for the rest of your life. Very simply, our baptism or renewal in the Jordan River that day was a powerful outward sign of the inward transformation in our life. While the physical act of baptism is performed outwardly, it is believed to signify the inward reception of God's grace through faith. It is not the act itself that saves, but the grace of God that saves.

After dropping a transformed Marilyn off, we then traveled north toward the Golan Heights near Mount Hermon, then on to Caesarea Philippi, positioned on the Mediterranean coast, and then further north to the Lebanese border.

It seemed everywhere we went there was an archaeological dig site, oftentimes sectioned off with a length of string or rope connecting small wooden posts, cautioning us from falling into the dig site. There were bits and pieces of ancient civilization everywhere. I remember wading into the saltwater at the beach amongst the rocks, near Caesarea Philippi and finding small square bits and pieces, about the size of a quarter, of ancient tile designed with beautiful mosaic colors. Some of this had to be thousands of years old and there it was discarded, as it washed up with the waves onto the shore—over and over. I wanted to take a few small tiles home with me as souvenirs, so I did. Outwardly, I was collecting souvenirs, inwardly I was remembering God's transforming grace. These were not the type of souvenirs you'd find in the marketplace, though there were plenty of opportunities for those. For me, I was witnessing God's grace in these small tiles being tossed around by the sea. It was a reminder of my own journey, being tossed around by the cares and concerns of the world—making a decision to turn from my former ways and embrace God's plan. There were several intact beautiful blue ones I especially liked. They reminded me of a clear blue sky on a peaceful sunlit day. The deep mysterious blue, not the dark angry charcoal blue that might appear before a storm.

Throughout much of our travels, we witnessed the continued evidence of the fighting and war between Israel and Palestine. There were pairs of soldiers on foot everywhere and small jeeps with a rear mounted sub-machine gun on patrol. It was a constant reminder of the turmoil.

Our guide explained that after high school, nearly all Israeli students must serve two to three years in the military. Basic training may last up to four months and the newly enlisted are taught the fundamentals of combat, military discipline, weapons training, and the philosophy of the Israeli Defense Forces. Young soldiers, usually patrolling in pairs, were seen everywhere we went, including the mall and marketplace in Jerusalem.

We were scheduled to spend our last three days in Jerusalem, the sacred city now shared by those practicing Judaism, Christianity, and Islam. It is one of the oldest cities in the world, located on a plateau in the Hebron Mountains between the Mediterranean and the Dead Sea. We arrived late due to traffic and had dinner afterward. The falafel, which is made of a mixture of ground chickpeas and spices, we ate together on the rooftop overlooking the old part of the city. We could see part of the Dome of the Rock and the Western Wall as the light grew dim over the city.

Our guide had made special arrangements for us to stay at a pilgrim house, called Ecce Homo, with the sisters of Notre Dame de Sion. The rooms were very small—like a cell, although comfortable, and clean. Everything in the ancient building was extremely old. It was overlooking the winding twisted cobblestone route, taken by Jesus on his way to be crucified. Tomorrow, we planned to walk that route, the Via Dolorosa, taking turns carrying a wooden cross. We were so fortunate to stay in this part of the old city. Not many do. It was breathtaking and transforming.

The Via Dolorosa is often called the "Way of Sorrow" or "Way of the Cross." This historic and spiritual journey began for us at what is now the site of the Antonia Fortress, where Jesus was condemned by Pontius Pilate. This marks the start of his grueling journey of suffering, carrying the horizontal piece of the cross on his shoulders amidst the crowds. As he moved through the streets, he bore the weight of the heavy wooden cross. The Bible does not specify the exact weight of Jesus' cross. Some historians estimate that the entire cross weighed around three-hundred pounds. The crossbeam is estimated to have weighed around ninety pounds.[5] The physical burden of carrying it to the place of execution symbolized the weight of humanity's sins that Jesus willingly took upon himself. For the crucifixion, Jesus was then led to a small hill outside the city gate, at a place of punishment reserved for criminals. He was crucified along with two others, one on his left and the other on his right. All three were brutally nailed through their hands and feet to the cross, and then raised upright, as they hung there in extreme agony for many hours. While on the cross, Jesus spoke to onlookers and to some of those who loved him.

One of the thieves who hung to his side hurled insults at him: "Are you not the Christ? Save yourself and us!" But the other rebuked him saying. "Do you not fear God, since you are under the same sentence of condemnation? And we indeed justly, for we are receiving the due reward of our deeds; but this man has done nothing wrong." The criminal pleaded, "Jesus, remember me when you come into your kingdom." And Jesus quickly said to him, "Truly, I say to you, today you will be with me in paradise" (Luke 23: 39–43). What a powerful encounter of love. God was willing to forgive this criminal just before he died. I wondered if that was similar to some of my cancer patients who, just before passing, came to believe that Jesus died for their sin. Some had asked that I remember them while I was in Jerusalem.

Father Rick Martignetti, describes this compelling event in his book, *Hidden Beauty*, where Jesus, even on the cross, never stopped loving us. He challenges the reader by saying:

> "We might think of it this way as Jesus was positioned on the cross between the two criminals. Satan tried all he could to make Jesus give up and stop loving. The tale of Jesus includes the story of the evil one who saw love coming and tried to stop him. It is as if Satan and his fallen angels said, 'we are greater than love and are going

---

5. Zugibe, *The Crucifixion of Jesus*, 41.

to prove it. Watch what we can do, watch us destroy love. We will hit love with confusion, humiliation, dishonor and sorrow. We will strike love, pierce love with a crown of thorns, beat love, and totally immerse love into intense suffering. We will fix love to a cross after ripping him back and forth with a whip like an animal. We will curse love, accuse him, condemn him, abandon him and see just how long it takes for love to stop loving.' But love never stopped loving. Cursed, condemned, dishonored, humiliated, love kept on loving. Even nailed to a cross with his last breath, Jesus Christ was more concerned about the souls of his persecutors than the state of his body. While dying on the cross Jesus looked out at his attackers and offered a prayer of forgiveness for them. He looked at the repentant criminal by his side and promised him paradise. Through such mercy, love kept on loving right up to the end and showed that he could never be stopped. In holding fast to his mission even in the face of an agonizing death on the cross, love emerged as the greatest power on earth. Love is greater than hate, greater than sin, greater than death, and greater than Satan, who's planned to destroy love backfired. Crucified love opened the gates of paradise inviting each of us, repented sinners to enter and find peace."[6]

After the crucifixion, Jesus' body was taken down from the cross and placed in a tomb. On the third day, which is celebrated as Easter, he was resurrected from the dead, seen by more than five-hundred witnesses.

Jesus' love changed everything. It had changed me. My faith was fairly new and this incredible experience strengthened it. Many of the places and events I had been reading about in the Bible became real. This story was very real. There was evidence that Jesus walked this earth, that he was raised from the tomb and died on Calvary. I was increasingly convinced that my redeemer had spent time in this little corner of the earth. My heart overflowed with hope and a deep sense of God's incredible love for me. What a powerful experience it was to visit Jerusalem. I was so blessed to

6. Martignetti, *Hidden Beauty*, 89–90.

have had the opportunity not only to visit the ancient culture but to experience so many unique and vivid places where Christianity began so long ago. I walked where Jesus had walked. How would I respond when I returned to Maine, my work and all my problems?

13

Skating on Thick Ice
1984

MY BROTHER AND HIS family were renting a house in the same neighborhood as Jeanne, allowing me to visit both in one evening. Their youngest child, David, was now walking around and climbing everything in sight. He was very quick. I was surprised how friendly and warm he was to me during my visits, reinforcing my joyful role as uncle. I now viewed these young versions of their mother and father with a different perspective.

Marked by the arrival of an unexpected package, I found myself confronted with the topic of marriage and divorce again. There were three small books wrapped together with a short introductory note. The arrival of one particular book by Charles Swindoll, *Striking the Original Match*, felt like a divine nudge urging me to reconsider my perceptions and desires. It contained some practical information and pointed out that even though I had been married before, there might be good reasons to consider marriage again.

After I plunged into the pages of the book, grappling with its insights for living, I found myself thinking more about Jeanne and her resilience. Despite the challenges she faced, she embraced change with steady determination—a strength I admired. She was spiritually more mature than I was, and her busy schedule of commitments only added to her allure, leaving me with lingering questions about striking the match.

I had experienced numerous radical changes. I was no longer wandering in the wilderness but instead traveling on a more stable road. Finding courage made change easier, although it came with its own costs. It was about the willingness to embark on a new journey toward understanding, love, and faith, even when the path is challenging or unclear. The book I received in the mail gave me the courage to risk thinking more seriously about change. It was just what I needed at the time. Interestingly, I had never signed up for or requested any books. The timing of the insight astonished me.

According to Brené Brown, a renowned author and speaker who highlights the connection between courage and vulnerability, change often requires risks. "It takes courage to confront our fears, face uncertainties, and make changes in our lives, which can be scary and daunting."[1]

When I thought about Jeanne, who seemed to be watching me from a distance, I often wondered if she was out of my league. There were two strikes against me—my newness to christianity and a previous marriage. She was not looking for a used car with a lot of miles on it. I wasn't without a past. But this theme or sense that I was a new creation, born again, with my slate wiped clean, continued to move through my mind encouraging me. This realization empowered me to embrace change and pursue bold possibilities.

I wasn't sure where this newfound courage came from. It was as if I was being pulled toward her. It was a gentle pull. It made it comfortable that she was easy to talk with. She is one of those rare types where there are few, if any, awkward pauses in the conversation. Author Richard Rohr describes some of the characteristics I identified in Jeanne in his book *Holy Spirit Baptism of Fire and Spirit*, "We sometimes can recognize people who have had a second baptism, not by water, but by the Holy Spirit. They tend to be loving. They tend to be exciting. They want to serve others, not just be served themselves. They forgive life itself for not being

---

1. Brown, *Courage in the midst of Change*, 01:15.

everything they once hoped for."[2] This perfectly described Jeanne. There was a specialness about her—perhaps she had experienced a second baptism that I was not aware of. I would ask her.

As winter moved in with its cold nights and occasional snow storm, we would sometimes run into each other on Sunday evenings among a small group of young adults from our church group. Everyone would gather on the Brunswick Mall to skate together, if the weather permitted. Brunswick's public works department would routinely flood the small flat grassy area off Main Street, a short, captivating walk from Bowdoin College. Many of us would often mingle with Bowdoin students who knew how to skate or witness those who were learning. Those learning would be awkwardly guiding or pushing a folding chair around the ice, holding on and trying desperately trusting their skates to remain upright. The chair actually helped stabilize them as they learned to balance. I thought that was a clever idea. Although, Jeanne did not need a chair to guide her on the ice—she was a veteran skater, better than me.

Having learned with my brother at an early age, I felt comfortable on the ice. In fact, he became the starting goalie as a junior for our high school hockey team. He and I always enjoyed skating and playing hockey together, especially on the local ponds. We practiced for hours, me shooting tennis balls at a make-shift goal—he guarded one end of the basement.

It was the perfect time to gather under the dim lighting on a cold winter night, especially after a snowstorm, where the trees surrounding the man-made rink would display the beauty of the fresh fallen snow weighing heavy on their limbs. I began to look forward to these weekly gatherings, especially if Jeanne was there.

On one occasion, only a few of us showed up to skate that night, giving me Jeanne all to myself. We skated together on the ice side by side, sometimes matching the rhythm of our stroke, gliding effortlessly together, losing track of time. The skating was smooth that night, and she was in a talkative mood as we circled the pond. She shared on a deeper level than she had in the past, confiding

---

2. Rohr, *Holy Spirit Baptism*, 1.

in me and offering uncomfortable details about her difficult days growing up in the mill town of Lewiston.

She explained at length how she was forced to grow up fast and learn to take responsibility for things around her, even as a young teenager. Her mother worked the second shift. Dad was a drinker, making the rounds on the way home from the shoe factory before settling in with a six pack of Budweiser. Others in her family depended on her, especially her three younger siblings. It was common in those days for the older sibling to set the table, get dinner ready and babysit the younger ones. We talked and skated together most of the night.

She shared a deeper, more vulnerable part of herself that day on the ice, and it made me want to hear more. I also shared about growing up on the poor side of the wealthy town of Barrington. After that night, I felt our friendship grew stronger. The pulling continued toward her—a desire to see her during the week, not wanting to wait, hoping the weather would remain cold enough to support the ice.

On other occasions later that winter, we would find ourselves skating on the Cathance River just as it emptied out of Bradley Pond in Topsham. There was a small group of four or five of us, all part of the Brunswick Mall group, that would gather on sunny Saturday mornings. That winter, the skating conditions were magical on the river. Earlier, the water level was considerably higher than normal that year. The ice had frozen perfectly amongst all the small trees and bushes that supported the banks of the river, doubling and sometimes tripling the skating area. We would effortlessly maneuver between the snow dusted trees and the small bushes before emerging on the clear expansive glassy area of the central part of river again, sometimes skating for more than a mile downstream. Conditions were like a winter wonderland, right out of a book: snow covered trees, brisk cold air and ice as smooth as glass.

Each encounter with Jeanne deepened my pull toward her, igniting a desire within me to explore the possibility of a deeper connection. Our shared moments on the ice, skating effortlessly amidst the winter landscape, became cherished memories. It was during these times that I found the courage to bare my soul, revealing the scars of my past, hidden secrets buried in the depths of my heart. I shared my sorted adventures of self-centeredness and my "prodigal son" experience. In my mind, I was taking a huge risk of being rejected.

She asked question after question as we moved along the central part of the river toward the pond. The ice that winter was so clean and extra thick from the cold temperatures. Would those conditions soon turn rough? Had I taken too big a risk by sharing my dark past? I left the river that day wondering just what would happen when I saw her next. I would not blame her if she skated away. I had unpacked most of my dirty, nasty baggage and past mistakes. It was like asking her to drink from a fire hose. It was difficult to share but healing. If she had been a priest, it would have been a good confession.

I shared with her how I had gotten so inwardly focused. I didn't care much about others, as my major theme in life was—it's all about me! I was only interested in various forms of immediate gratification and self indulgence. In California, every night after work, it was time to party; lots of drinking and smoking weed. And on weekends, it intensified starting earlier in the day.

As the weeks followed, we would see each other at church or a friend's house. She thanked me for sharing that day on the river. It meant a lot to her that I trusted her. She reminded me that in Christ, I was a new creation and that God had a special plan for me. I was happy she had not totally rejected me. What was that plan? This plan God had for me—did it include her?

After the weather warmed, our ice skating on the river diminished. Jeanne was always on my mind, every day now—I couldn't shake it. A few weeks later, while praying before work, a poetic riff came to mind effortlessly as I thought of her. I kept writing as the words appeared in my mind's eye.

> *Like a flower that rests at night.*
> *It waits for the morning sun,*
> *patient and still.*

Skating on Thick Ice

It's beauty and loveliness speak for themselves,
opening and smiling at the world,
taking in the sun and,
reflecting its beauty,
for all who see.

She's made in God's image.
I'm sure at a glance you can tell
she speaks of his love,
It's written as in a book—plain to see.

Throughout the weeks that followed, she came to mind during the day. At night I thought of her. What was she doing right now? The world around me had suddenly become more intense, colorful, and brighter. The blues were bluer—so many shades of green, and the sun—it felt brighter and warmer.

There were times of sneaking up to her car in the evening and leaving a note, telling her I was thinking of her. The new Post-It Notes were just the right thing for this because you could stick the note in an obscure place like on the rearview mirror, or under a book on the seat. A little surprise waiting to be discovered. My playful spirit was fully engaged.

Later in our relationship, my Post-It Notes became short letters and little cards I would leave in her car or send in the mail. This was before cell phones and email. On the outside of the envelope, I might write something like: "The contents of this envelope were chosen with great care on an individual basis. Nothing artificial has been added, only the choicest ingredients; one-hundred percent pure love." Inside, I would reveal some of my medical background by saying, "If symptoms such as happiness, smiling, and in extreme cases of excessive joy develop, please contact the Great Physician!"

Our courtship lasted only a few months before we decided on an early October wedding. I had wanted to ask Jeanne's dad for his blessing to marry his eldest daughter, but he had passed away a year earlier from lung cancer. So, I made a lunch date with her mother instead to seek her blessing before I proposed. I wanted to honor her. Irene could hardly contain herself when I broke the news that her first born was getting married. As we agreed, she could not tell anyone, including her own mother, until I proposed to her daughter later that week with the small diamond ring purchased on credit.

Our engagement flew by. It seemed as though I now had so many additional aunts, uncles and cousins, all of French background. Her family was huge. I had problems remembering names and whose side of the family the relative belonged to. Every weekend I was introduced to someone else in my growing family. Wedding plans came together smoothly, with a borrowed chalet in Vermont to begin our honeymoon, before moving on to the romantic City of Quebec just over the border.

We surprised everyone by standing on each side of the large doors to St John's Church and greeted each guest as they entered. I remember being full of unending joy that day. People kept commenting that the bride and groom were not to see each other before exchanging vows, but that we looked radiant standing together at the entrance to the church. This was our "receiving line," welcoming everyone into our new life together. I could not stop smiling.

14

Meeting Ernie

1985

WE BEGAN RENTING A renovated apartment in Brunswick before we were married. I would be living there alone until October. Despite its clean and tidy appearance, the older building had some hidden challenges, including outdated plumbing and insufficient insulation. The winter was particularly cold, making it difficult to stay warm with electric heat while trying to stick to our budget. Our landlord initially seemed friendly and caring, but like the apartment, he had hidden issues that made him seem colder the more we got to know him.

Buying a home in the eighties was challenging, especially for young first-time buyers. Interest rates were very high, peaking around 16 percent before gradually declining to about 13 percent in 1985. These ridiculous rates made borrowing very costly, impacting everyone's ability to afford a home. Despite this, Jeanne and I eagerly explored the market to see what we could afford together.

The economic conditions made recovery from the recession difficult, as the Fed's tight monetary policies aimed to combat inflation that was near 13 percent in the 1980s. Gas shortages from the seventies, due to reduced oil production in the Middle East, further strained the economy. Long lines at gas stations and high fuel prices became common, forcing more people to carpool and tighten their budget.

Jeanne worked for a real estate lawyer, performing title searches at the city of Bath's Registry of Deeds. The red-hot market kept her busy, often requiring overtime. I didn't see her as much, but we were saving money. She was seen as an outstanding employee, and her boss even offered to cover the cost of our title search if we ever found a house.

After several meetings with our real estate broker, viewing and evaluating small and medium-sized starter homes, we were shocked and disappointed by what was available. It seemed we couldn't afford much or get much value for what we could afford. We considered waiting to save more or try to increase our income. I thought about finding a part-time job at night or on weekends. Most of the houses we viewed needed maintenance and repair, and the small lots offered little privacy. We understood these were "starter homes."

While shopping for winter boots at L.L. Bean, I was complaining to my sister-in-law Janet about the housing market when we unexpectedly ran into Jim, a friend from our old church group in New Gloucester. He gave me a big hug and happily exclaimed, "Hey Dennis. It's been a while. How have you been? I heard you were getting married." After recovering from his big hug, I said, "Jim, good to see you again. I'm doing great. What have you been up to?" Jim, smiling, responded, "I've got some exciting news. I'm working on a new project as a real estate developer and have my second development underway not too far from you." With my interest peeked, I responded, "Really? I can't believe you're telling me this." Jim was excited now. "Yeah, we bought an eighteen-acre parcel adjacent to the Bisson Farm on Meadow Road, and it includes that older brick home on the corner of Meadow Road and Maine Route 201, part of it dating back to the late 1780s." He went on about the brick house, "The original house is on the old Augusta Road, which used to be part of a stagecoach route when the road was made of sand and clay, connecting Portland and Augusta.

Meeting Ernie

The interesting thing is that the building served as an overnight stop for passengers well before the railroad came along. I'm really fascinated by its history. I bet it could tell stories"

Jim was a tall, reserved man who stood out not only for his stature but also for his solid character. A quiet presence, Jim was known for his fairness and integrity in business. A man who let his actions speak louder than words, driven by a sincere desire to help others. He displayed plenty of enthusiasm as a new developer.

I was eager to find out more about this new subdivision, responding, "You always did appreciate history. What are your plans with the land? Are you doing a sub-division?" He responded, "If you and Jeanne are interested, my wife and I would love to meet with you and discuss things. Handing me a smart looking business card, Jim grinned enthusiastically, "Excellent. Let's get in touch soon. I'd be happy to help build you the perfect home."

Later that week, we made an appointment to meet for coffee at the Kopper Kettle in Topsham. Over the years they have provided customers with a family-owned place to have breakfast and lunch, offering good hearty food and homemade bread. We were both excited about the food and our meeting. Jim was new to real estate development. I trusted his kind and gentle spirit as he outlined the details of the new project, using a detailed map and invited us to look at one of the two lots available on Jesse Road. After our Saturday morning breakfast, we eagerly drove over to the land and walked the two lots, which did indeed have a stream running through the back portion of each. It was picturesque.

The first lot abutted Meadow Road and the old stagecoach home, with limited space for building due the sloping hill and boggy terrain near the stream. The second lot was larger, with the stream further back surrounded by beautiful tall white pines near a natural spring. This lot had a poured foundation from a previous project that had fallen through weeks earlier, requiring us, if we did purchase it, to build a cape-style home.

Days later, after some discussion, Jeanne and I were all in and agreed to purchase the foundation lot, excited by the prospect of starting construction before we were married and the cold Maine weather set in. To reduce the overall cost, we committed to completing all the interior painting, exterior staining and landscaping, saving us about a thousand dollars. We also planned to leave the upstairs bedrooms and bathroom unfinished, intending to complete them later as funds allowed.

We soon found ourselves meeting with Ernie, an overweight, middle-aged Italian who ran a mortgage company out of Portland. He was a friend of Jim's and was smooth and easy to talk to. Ernie enjoyed commanding your attention by telling jokes with a cigarette hanging out of his mouth, reminding me of a guy I knew in Rhode Island who enjoyed making a deal and would not rest until it was done. As we sat nervously around the small table, he collected the necessary paperwork and explained the financing details at 14 percent. Rates were high everywhere, but this was the best deal he had to offer us. I was new to financing, but Jeanne was not. It all sounded possible as long as we could afford the mortgage payment.

For several weeks we were asked to supply more paperwork proving that I did actually work at the community college, that Jeanne worked at the law office and we would actually be gifted five-thousand dollars from my parents toward the down payment. Just when I thought we had completed the required documents, Ernie's secretary would call again and demand another piece of evidence. We complied with every request, sometimes more than once, because that's what we had to do. I was using a fax machine at the hospital to communicate with Ernie's secretary. The state-of-the-art hospital fax machine saved me a bundle of time. US mail was slow, but faster than the old stage coach represented by Jim's new property.

Our next meeting included Jim, Ernie, Jeanne and me. Ernie reviewed the thick folder of paperwork in detail and scrutinized each of our expenses. Ernie was concerned about our application. According to his company's lending policy, the borrower's total mortgage expenses could not exceed a certain percentage of their total income. Ours did. One particular line item on our expense report included an amount we donated each month to charities and our church, which was about ten percent of our income.

Meeting Ernie

He stared intently at both of us with his cigarette dangling. Ernie inquired, "Did we really give this amount to charities and is this something we were willing to exclude from the application?" He suggested we cut back on this for a while and not report it. "If we did remove this amount from the expense report," as Ernie's grin widened, "no one would be the wiser—it would be just between us and just for a while."

Jim was squirming in his seat at this news, as this was looking like it would be strike two for him on the foundation property. Initially, he had taken on the costs of pouring the foundation and site work himself, a rookie mistake for a real estate developer, making him responsible for the interest on the loan each month. Less profit, in the long run for him.

Jim looked at Ernie with a weak smile (almost like a preplanned clue) and the two of them spent the next fifteen minutes taking turns reminding us of all the benefits of homeownership, the financing we were receiving and anything else they could think of in an effort to close the deal that day. All we needed to do was sign on the dotted line.

All we needed to do was deny the fact that we donated money to the church, as a tithe. We believed it was a responsibility we desired to continue. It was only one-tenth of the money we received. Ninety percent of the funds left over was ours to spend anyway we wanted in supporting our lifestyle.

The room grew quiet and the meeting with Ernie concluded. We were left with the impression that if we removed the amount we donated each month from the finance report, we would then qualify for the mortgage, otherwise our application would be denied. Ernie was very sorry and Jim was beside himself. Jim even tried to persuade us further in the parking lot before we all departed from Portland. We had three days to think about it.

Nothing changed over the next three days. I explained to Ernie later that we did not feel right removing that amount from the finance report we had submitted with our mortgage application. We were all disappointed there would be no house to move into. No sale for Jim and nothing for Ernie.

Our faith would be challenged. I was reminded of the passage in Paul's letter to the Hebrews (Heb 11:1). "Now faith is the assurance of things hoped for, the conviction of things not seen." We were certainly hoping for a new home, but at this point, the financing door had closed. As difficult as it was to maintain a certainty in what we did not see, we wanted to believe that God had a plan for us. Perhaps a different house, another mortgage?

A miraculous change occurred several days later. Ernie called at work. I recognized his unmistakable deep Italian voice. He excitedly explained that he had felt a strange urge to make things right for us, as we seemed like a nice young couple and he wanted to help. "I couldn't get you off my mind", he explained. "I spent parts of the next few days exhausting all my options trying to make a conventional mortgage loan work for you. The numbers would just did not work. But, I found something that might work."

I could tell he was motivated when he raised his deep scratchy voice and said, "I found some loan money under a new program administered by the Maine State Housing Authority for first time home buyers." He indicated that I should make a separate application with just my income and see what would happen, as we were not yet married. Making an appointment in Portland, we met later that week to explore this new option.

With another cigarette dangling from his lips, he managed a smile as he welcomed us to discuss the new terms. He was beaming and quickly shared the details. Instead of the traditional twenty percent needed for a down payment with a conventional mortgage, our new terms as first-time home buyers required only 5 percent down. The interest rate was 9.9 percent for our thirty-year fixed mortgage instead of 13.9 percent. The news overwhelmed us. We were going to build a house together. God had provided a way where there seemed to be no way. This was truly incredible.

Our hearts were filled with gratitude. The journey to this point had been filled with all kinds of obstacles. There were times when the dream of owning a home felt like a distant, unattainable goal due to financial struggles, market uncertainties, and personal doubts. Yet, here we stood, on the brink of an amazing adventure together.

Reflecting on the events that had led us to this breakthrough, we couldn't help but marvel at how things had fallen into place. It wasn't just luck or coincidence; it felt like divine intervention. We wondered if God was honoring our decision to keep all the items on the finance report, staying honest and transparent even when it seemed easier to cut corners.

Jim was as happy about the final approval on our new loan application as we were. He was with us throughout the entire financial challenge and said he had never seen anything like it before. He was calling it the "Jesse Road Miracle." Within just two months of signing, the house was buttoned up for winter. Work moved forward inside. They were building walls, running the electricity and plumbing. We had purchased a large wood stove at a local hardware store and installed it in the basement just as winter was setting in, feeding it daily.

Within three years, we were considering changing the name of Jesse Road to Leaver Lane. My brother Don and his family completed their home across the street and moved in with their three children about a year after us. They used the same builder. My brother, an engineer, carefully designed his home to accommodate his growing family and even angled the house on his one-acre lot to take maximum advantage of the sun's path over his portion of Jesse Road.

My parents would be next. In a sense, we were creating a type of family compound. Due in part to the housing shortages in New England, my parents, who lived in the house where they raised us near one-hundred-acre cove in Barrington, were selling. Interestingly, they were approached by a neighbor's daughter asking if they wanted to sell. I grew up with Cheryl, who lived two houses down from us. She boldly approached my folks, knocked on the door and told them she wanted to live next to her mother and father on Mason Road.

After the Barrington paperwork was signed, my parents were still shocked at how much they came away with. It was not long after the neighbor's knock that they were meeting with Jim about the last lot on Jesse Road. It was the very lot Jeanne and I had walked near the top of the road, probably the least desirable of the eight lots in Jim's second subdivision development—Meadow View Estates. There was really only one place to locate my parents small ranch on the property. My mom and dad were fine with that. They were just happy to be moving to Maine where most of their grandchildren lived.

They settled right into the family compound overlooking the Bisson farm on Meadow Road, a beautiful stretch of farmland that has always been productive in raising their four-hundred or more head of beef cattle and dairy cows on their five-hundred acres, bordering the Cathance River. We all would come to recognize what type of fertilizer they were spreading in the spring and fall, especially if the wind was out of the north.

It was so good to have my parents living down the street from us, especially as our family grew. Before long, we had three boys and my brother had four children right across the street. They were in a perfect time of their life to be surrounded by grandchildren. My mother had not worked in many years and my dad enjoyed retirement and now a new home. They were both ready to help the two Jesse Road families with childcare, odd jobs around the house, and organize family celebrations.

It was a perfect fit for Jeanne and me. Having grandparents in the neighborhood, walking distance to their house, allowed each of our children to regularly visit. They kept individual treats in a cupboard designed to lure each of the grandchildren down for more frequent visits. They had something sweet or salty for each of them. Daniel and Aaron enjoyed playing cards and munching on the treats. If my youngest son Jude lost his temper or became mad about something, he would stomp off down Jesse Road, proclaiming he was leaving and might be back later. Grampy usually had some Pringles stored in his cupboard to comfort Jude. Aaron soon became a die-hard Red Sox fan like his grandfather.

It all started with Jim and Ernie—two people who worked hard using their skills to help a young couple buy their first house—more families followed. They both demonstrated a genuine desire to help. Ernie was willing to take a risk and go the extra mile to find a mortgage for us even in a hot real estate market. This allowed both of them to connect deeply with us creating a ripple effect. In essence, this ripple effect served as a reminder that our choices matter and that we can influence others around us, often in ways we may not fully realize.

15

The Ripple Effect
1985

THE COMMUNITY COLLEGE CAMPUS where I worked was located on the rocky coast of Maine at the site of the old Fort Preble. Many of the brick buildings had been remodeled, much like myself. The fort, which was designed to protect the Portland harbor, was built in the early 1800s, expanded over the years, and very active during World War II. The red brick buildings of the old ocean-side fort are famous for their solid construction and historical significance. Each building features thick, weathered brick walls that have stood firm despite many coastal storms. The slate roofs, with their dark, durable tiles, provide a striking contrast to the surroundings.

I found it interesting that while my father was serving in the 82nd Airborne in Europe during World War II, soldiers were also stationed at Fort Preble, now the site of Southern Maine Community College. Many of the buildings, such as the officers' quarters or the hospital, had been renovated into classroom space, and some heavy artillery fortifications were still visible along the rocky coast. Many of the underground bunkers were accessible. What a stunning location, which included a spark plug shaped lighthouse guarding the harbor, a good size sandy beach, and walking trails connecting the eighty acres. The views of Portland harbor and surrounding islands attracted numerous visitors, especially during the summer months. This picturesque location became my second home for over thirty-five years. It included daily commutes back and forth across the "Million Dollar Bridge", with its breathtaking views of Portland's harbor. I tried to carry some reading material—mostly work related stuff, like journal articles about cancer or something I might review for a lab or lecture. I needed something to reflect on or help pass the time when the bridge was up, allowing a large tanker ship into or out of the harbor. The unplanned fifteen-minute delay always seemed to occur when I was in a hurry.

I remembered saying to myself that first week on campus, "I feel very different." I don't quite know how to put it into words. Perhaps my pride is surfacing now that I have this position at the college. My new attire, consisting of a freshly pressed shirt, tie, and new pants reminded me of this. Feeling different was likely a result of winning this new job and all the uncertainties associated with it. It felt so daunting, and everything about the new role was demanding, but exciting.

There was a distinct, overwhelming feeling surrounding me at the hospital and on campus. The job required me to divide my time between both places. I was a smidgeon more comfortable at the hospital where I had worked for several years. Teaching and creating lesson plans were new to me. I soon learned from others that teaching involves several key steps to ensure effective learning. First, I needed to formulate clear and measurable objectives that define what students should know or do by the end of the lesson. Next, I was supposed to develop a detailed lesson plan that included instructional strategies, a list of materials or equipment needed, and identify activities designed to achieve these objectives. I learned from some of my veteran colleagues, the plan should also cater to diverse learning styles and include engaging content. Finally, I needed to incorporate some form of evaluation, such as quizzes, tests, or assignments, to assess my students' understanding and measure their achievement. I was learning to do this on the go.

I did not have a teaching degree or any formal education in this area. Dr. Hannemann often reminded me, "At your core, Dennis, you are a fine teacher. I have seen how you interact with both patients and students." My oldest brother Robert, who had his own consulting firm, also encouraged me and reminded me that the art of teaching is learning what not to teach.

Most people at the hospital, including some therapists and nurses, said I should apply for the new job. They repeatedly told me, "You'd be good at it. You seem to really enjoy working with students, helping them understand how to treat the patient with compassion. They like you. You're always drawing helpful diagrams to demonstrate some concept, especially as it involves geometry and how all the radiation beam angles intersect."

Oftentimes, I found myself off in a corner, helping a student understand why we were treating a breast cancer patient from multiple angles or why a prostate cancer patient needed immobilization in the pelvic area to prevent any slight movement during treatment. Most treatment beams entered the body from numerous precisely calculated angles, centered around a single point, usually in the center of the tumor volume. The students didn't get much one-on-one teaching in the clinic; they were expected to learn by observation and asking questions. That may work for some. Unfortunately, most of those in the clinic believed the learning process for students happened by osmosis or diffusion. They actually believed that students would absorb knowledge and understanding if they stood close by and observed intently alongside the doctor or therapist.

A practical example of diffusion is like taking a paper towel and placing it on a flat surface just touching a measured amount of water—then watching the liquid slowly move into the paper towel—like magic. The water is slowly absorbed without moving the paper towel, transitioning from an area of high concentration (the pool of water) to an area of low concentration (the dry paper towel). The water moves slowly but effortlessly. This did not always happen when transferring knowledge and understanding in the clinic. It might. I felt students needed more one-on-one instruction, perhaps a type of facilitated diffusion, where there was a helping hand. Teaching for me was challenging at first, but became exciting, especially when the proverbial light went on.

My decision to move from the clinical setting at the hospital to the academic setting was a difficult one. I really loved working at the hospital, ministering to each patient, getting to know them and their disease processes, helping them with questions about treatment and side effects, and sometimes praying for them. For some, we would talk about what God was or wasn't doing with them at the time. For me, ministering meant using my radiation therapy skills while combining prayer and spiritual direction for each patient who was open to that approach. Not everyone wanted to include God in their fight against cancer, but more did than I initially expected. I felt that every interaction was an opportunity to influence and be influenced, to make a difference, and to contribute to a positive change in the life of my patient.

For example, I remember a middle-aged woman named Betty, who had been diagnosed with a particularly aggressive form of breast cancer. She was initially hesitant about any spiritual aspect of her treatment, focusing solely on the technical components of the medical procedure. However, as we spent more time together and moved further along in her treatment, discussing her fears and hopes, she began to open up about her spiritual struggles. We would see each other every day and sometimes strike up conversations about faith and doubt, about finding peace in the midst of suffering. One day, she asked me to pray with her before her first chemotherapy session directly after her radiation treatment. Later, it became a routine, and I watched as her spirit grew stronger, even as her body battled the disease.

On another occasion, a particularly outgoing patient mentioned the importance of prayer in everything he did. I listened carefully. God was important to him, as his family and friends were all praying for him around the clock. He also wanted to include all the doctors and therapists administering the radiation treatments in his prayers. We connected immediately. He was authentic and real. We discussed the importance of prayer, especially as he fought his battle. He looked directly into my eyes, rested his hand on my shoulder, and said, "You must speak to God a great deal—I imagine you get down on your knees and ask for guidance every day because of the seriousness of your work. All of us patients are fighting for our lives and depend on you and the rest of the team to do everything you can in your power to help us." This revelation opened me even wider to what God was doing. I realized that part of me had been acting on my own. I needed to heed his advice and pray for more guidance in my work. It was one of those fierce conversations. It changed me.

At that time, the American Cancer Society estimated that about thirty-five percent of all cancer patients in the United States, treated with surgery, radiation, and/or chemotherapy or some combination of these three, would be cured of their disease. This statistic served as a stark reminder of the limitations of medical science in the early eighties. A majority of people, unfortunately, would not experience a cure. The eighties were a period of transformation, where oncology was making significant strides, yet the survival rate indicated that much progress was still needed. Many of us worked hard to carefully combine the positive effects of surgery and radiation therapy or the addition of chemotherapy. These separate departments, found in most cancer hospitals, explored and tested ways to collaborate, instead of treating the disease independently, much the way it had been done up to that point. Collaborative efforts between oncologists, researchers, and other healthcare providers were crucial in sharing knowledge, pooling resources, and developing more effective treatment protocols, ultimately leading to improved patient outcomes. Strong families are good at pooling their resources in helping one another to create better outcomes.

For those patients who would not survive their disease, the role of healthcare providers extended far beyond traditional treatment. We would provide more than just medical care, offering comfort, a listening ear, and effective pain relief. Creating a supportive environment where patients could feel free to express their fears and hopes, ensuring they felt heard and understood was essential. Palliative care was not just about managing physical symptoms, but also addressing emotional and psychological needs, assisting patients and their families to navigate the challenging journey with dignity and compassion. It seemed, at that time, everyone knew someone close to them that had cancer.

So why would I leave the hospital to move across town to Southern Maine Community College? Maine Medical Center was the primary clinical education center for most of the radiation therapy students and the largest hospital in Maine. This is where all the unusual and difficult cases from other parts of the state were sent to be treated. Outside of Boston, Maine Medical Center, which included the Barbara Bush Children's Hospital, treated nearly all the pediatric cancer cases in Maine.

It was a good friend of mine, Trip, who helped guide my decision to consider moving in this new direction. He was given that name as a young boy because he was the third Joseph in his family. They thought he needed his own identity. He was so intriguing spiritually, a Harvard graduate in business who loved God with all his heart, mind, and soul. He often preached the gospel, and if necessary, used words—a saying often attributed to St Francis of Assisi. Most everyone liked Trip. He was quiet, good looking, trim and walked the walk. He had a personal relationship with Jesus, was humble, and tried to obey God.

Trip never married, seeking instead to serve as a single. He felt the unmarried man was concerned how to please the Lord. But the married man is anxious about worldly things, how to please his wife, and his interests were divided (1 Cor 7:33). He chose to be undivided.

Seeking God's direction through prayer and service to others, he became a powerful mentor for me. I liked hanging out with him. He shared with me one cold autumn day, as I was describing what had happened at last week's prayer meeting and how it related to my difficulties in deciding about a new job at the college. He encouraged me to pursue God's direction, pray more often and try to listen intensely in a contemplative spirit.

I remember, as we walked along the trail that week following the banks of the Cathance river up toward Bradley Pond, Trip paused and looked directly into my eyes, "Perhaps you might think of this new teaching role in a way that would multiply your efforts—sort of like multiplying the loaves. This is where Jesus can take our small scanty gifts and mysteriously increases them to feed others."

He continued, "You could potentially increase your effectiveness interacting with thirty to forty cancer patients a day, Dennis, by raising up and teaching other students to treat patients in the same way that you have, with great love." He pondered for a moment, looking very serious, as if he were actually hearing from God, and continued, "Even if you graduated just ten other students in your lifetime who thought and believed like yourself—then over time, you would, in a way, affect three to four hundred cancer patients a day with great love and compassion." There was a long silence as we contemplated the pristine dark river moving slowly past us. Something in my heart was hearing this message flow deeper into my being. This ripple, or multiplication effect could become very powerful.

Interested, I looked up the Bible story about the multiplication of the loaves and fishes. It's a miracle described in all four Gospels. In the story, Jesus takes five loaves of bread and two fish offered by a young boy. After blessing the food, he begins breaking it into pieces, and miraculously, the food multiplies until everyone in the crowd of more than five-thousand has eaten their fill. Remarkably, twelve baskets of leftovers are gathered after everyone has eaten (Luke 9:13–17). This compelling story illustrates God's generous provision, showing us that when we give whatever we have, no matter how small, it can be multiplied or increased to meet the needs of many. In the story, Jesus not only addressed their physical needs but also transformed their hearts, demonstrating the power of faith and love.

As I look back, I think this eye-opening conversation marked a critical time in my walk. Several things began to change. This fierce encounter with Trip opened doors to unplanned opportunities. It shifted my perspective as it led me down a fresh new path.

The Ripple Effect

I felt moved by an inner force to embrace this new teacher role at the college. I wasn't afraid anymore. It was one of those fierce conversations you have once in a great while, with someone you trust, and later look back upon it with different eyes. This was one of those conversations. My heart was moved to raise up a new breed of radiation therapists to work with cancer patients—embracing precision, accuracy and great love—helping to cure patients and minimize the effects from treatment. I felt that we could move the needle in curing more cancer patients.

It wasn't long before I said "yes" to this new challenge by filling out the application at the community college and submitting the required references. There were only a few applicants for the job, and the search committee offered me the position, even without a teaching degree. What I did possess was a wealth of clinical experience, a desire to teach the student, and a unique understanding of treating cancer patients from the clinical experience gained in Providence, Boston, and California.

That powerful conversation with Trip that day would change my life dramatically and along with that, many others. Wow!

Susan Scott, author of numerous books on communication, leadership, and love, emphasizes the power of meaningful and authentic conversations. These conversations have the potential to be powerful and life-changing. She points out in her book, *Fierce Conversations; Achieving Success at Work and in Life One Conversation at a Time*: "While no single conversation is guaranteed to transform a company, a relationship, or a life, any single conversation can. Speak and listen as if this is the most important conversation you will ever have with this person. It could be. Participate as if it matters. It does."[1]

Having fierce conversations can be risky and unpredictable, yet may have effects we are unaware of until sometime later. While not every conversation will lead to dramatic change, the potential for any single conversation to do so is always present, highlighting the significance and importance of the interactions we have.

---

1. Scott, *Fierce Conversations*, 1.

God was unfolding a plan for me, and at the time I wasn't aware of where the plan would lead. My faith would be stretched and tested over and over. My new teaching role would eventually grow stronger affecting others. A good number of graduates would settle in Maine and more would move away to other cities becoming a powerful, loving presence in the lives of the cancer patient.

Trip continued to remind me of my role as teacher and mentor, "Remember, Dennis, Jesus was embracing a new direction when he gathered his twelve disciples, often teaching them with direct instruction and using the power of stories and engaging parables. Teaching by demonstrating practical lessons about faith and compassion, his followers gradually grew in their understanding—although some were slow to get the message. The three-year training period prepared the disciples to grow into a group of hand-picked figures of the early Christian church, multiplying the teachings of Jesus long after he was arrested and taken into custody."

Through the power of the Holy Spirit, they taught and lived out Jesus' message, similar to the multiplication of the loaves and fishes, eventually taking the message to distant lands in Europe, Asia and Africa. All but one would eventually die as martyrs for their faith.

The disciples too had accepted their new role after learning from their teacher. Actually, it became a life-changing career path for each of them. They too would raise up others, teaching as Jesus did. As Jesus was departing to heaven after the resurrection, he approached them and told them, "All authority in heaven and on earth has been given to me. Go therefore and make disciples of all nations, baptizing them in the name of the Father and of the Son and of the Holy Spirit" (Matt 28:18–19). He was sending them out on their own—to go and make a difference.

Not all, but some of my students would carry the same commitment to "go make a difference." My role became a means of creating a ripple effect, ensuring that more radiation therapists would touch additional lives beyond my direct reach. Having that type of seed planted in my heart was a powerful motivator to serve and love others.

16

Multiplying the Loaves
1994

THE CONCEPT OF MULTIPLYING the loaves, like Jesus' miracle, is often metaphorically applied to teaching, emphasizing the impact of sharing knowledge. By fostering a collaborative learning environment, encouraging curiosity, and using diverse teaching methods, a single person can inspire and educate beyond their initial reach. This ripple effect empowers students to become knowledge bearers themselves, magnifying their impact as they share insights with peers, patients, and future generations, thus perpetuating the cycle of learning and growth.

My years as an educator were challenging at first, but they became more effective as God worked through me and in me, helping others harness their inner strength to overcome challenges and obstacles. As the years passed, I grew in my understanding of what God had planned long ago. I had said "yes," even when I wasn't sure where it would take me. There were many times when I stumbled and learned from my mistakes. Eventually, with the help of other mentors, I earned a graduate degree and went on to teach for over three decades. There were times along that road I wanted to throw in the towel, perhaps try something different.

It's hard to believe my journey is nearing its end. I am preparing to finish running my own race. Now, in retirement, the level ground is easier to manage and navigate. This is especially true after I turned away from my self centered California days and my intense pursuit of happiness.

Lately, I've been focused on moving away from the demands of the false self—the self that adjusts to fit in with or please others. It often leads me to disconnect from my true feelings—the part of me that embraces vulnerability and my inner values. I now try to surround myself with people who appreciate, support, and encourage me. They help me when I encounter difficulties. Self-reflection, through prayer and journaling, has been important in understanding my inner-self and what really matters to me.

Richard Rohr, a Franciscan priest, describes the search for this true self in his book *Immortal Diamond*:

> "When the body is all you think you are; no wonder you are afraid of dying. It is all you know and have—if you have not discovered your soul, that is. The False Self is terrified of death because it knows this mental ego that it calls 'myself' will die and cannot find any long-term alternative to it, so it works for the short term instead. The False Self has no substance, no permanence, no vitality, only various forms of immediate gratification."[1]

I still, on occasion, fall into the habits of immediate gratification. Although I like to think I am getting better at recognizing this and understanding the constant attention my physical body wants.

After retiring, I taught part-time for several years, until COVID hit us all. Before retiring, the students I worked with mostly fell into two groups: anatomy & physiology students who needed the course to gain admission into nursing, radiography, or another health science program, and radiation therapy students. Most of my early years at the college were spent teaching and shaping a small group of radiation therapy students each year, while my later years were focused on anatomy & physiology students. Little did I know how my efforts would be multiplied when I first transitioned

---

1. Rohr, *Immortal Diamond*, 143.

from the hospital setting, to the academic world of teaching, speaking, and eventually writing about radiation therapy.

Early in my career, I began speaking at conferences, writing journal articles, and serving in my professional organizations. I enjoyed writing. And then, to my amazement and many others, especially my family, I wrote a textbook. This new project was much bigger than me, but filled my spirit with great passion to move it forward. In the *Principles and Practice of Radiation Therapy* textbook, co-authored with Charles Washington, the dedication reads:

> "To those who have run and continue to run the race against cancer. We sincerely hope that those who read this work will grow in the knowledge and understanding necessary to provide direction, care, and compassion to their patients, family, and supportive friends. Let us not grow tired in running our own race, but instead encourage those around us."[2]

The book was specifically written to guide students, unify our radiation therapy community from California to Maine, and contribute to the body of knowledge. We desired to encourage educators and students by providing a textbook written by radiation therapists specifically for the radiation therapy community.

The idea of writing a book like this had to be inspired by the Holy Spirit. And it was. In high school, I earned mostly 'C's' in English. I didn't even like writing because it was difficult, and I never seemed to come up with anything that sounded worthwhile or meaningful.

Interestingly, when I first attended the University of Rhode Island, I was placed in a remedial writing class to help me pass the composition class required for graduation. I must have been high that day or just tested poorly on the entrance exam for English, so I was plugged into this class of about twelve. I think we all needed to learn to write better. This professor had a powerful approach, which was just what I needed. He, too, had a gift for multiplying the loaves. I must say, this was a gratifying class that taught me to

---

2. Washington and Leaver, *Principles and Practice of Radiation Therapy*, vi.

write better. Passing the course with a "B", I enjoyed writing for the first time. I actually looked forward to going to class. The professor cared about his teaching, and wanted to make a difference. And he did.

Dr. Hannemann cared deeply about what he did as a physician. He too made a difference, as a powerful mentor and an example of what it means to lay one's life down for Christ. I was amazed to learn that he attended almost all his patients' funerals—the ones that fought hard, but did not make it. On occasion, we prayed together when I encountered difficulties, always seeking insight and direction.

After teaching radiation therapy students at the college for several years, I remember proclaiming to Dr. Hannemann, "I am going to write a book one of these days. I am sick and tired of teaching from so many different sources. There is nothing out there for students." I went on to tell him, "What we did have was a couple of good physics chapters from a book geared to teaching physicists. There was also a chapter or two from a radiation biology textbook we used. And then we had a couple of large, expensive textbooks to choose from that were designed to teach medical students about the various types of cancer, such as lymphoma, breast and prostate cancer. All of those books were not written with the radiation therapist in mind."

The radiation oncology doctor and therapist work closely together to treat the cancer patient. The radiation therapist is an essential part of the team interacting with the patient every single day, administering a small portion of the entire radiation dose needed to control the specific type of cancer. The treatment process must be both accurate and precise to deliver the prescribed dose effectively, aiming to control the disease while minimize the side effects. The therapist is often the go-to person in helping the patient cope with any emotional stress and side effects from the treatment or disease.

Early on in my teaching career, I was responsible for educating most of the radiation therapists who would end up working in a hospital or clinic in Maine, New Hampshire or northern

Massachusetts. We covered the entire region, which included maintaining key relationships in numerous clinical sites from Manchester to Presque Isle. Some graduates would go on to work in Boston, New York and other large cities.

In an effort to gather information on what it would take to write a book, I reached out to several authors of college textbooks, all in health science fields such as nuclear medicine, radiography, and nursing. I made a number of phone calls and was amazed at how forthcoming authors were in sharing the difficulties and the lengthy process they endured to get their book published. One individual I spoke with more than once was extremely encouraging and helpful. We talked about developing an outline, sample chapters, and a detailed proposal. She even shared information about the small amount of royalties you would earn. A meaningful book was going to take a long time—years.

I wasn't going to pursue this book project for the royalties, but the money would be helpful in raising three children on a teacher's salary. Interestingly, many of my graduates were earning more money than I was as a college professor at the time. Graduates were generally in high demand because there always seemed to be a shortage of radiation therapists.

Partway through the process of developing a book proposal, I became aware that another radiation therapy professor in Texas was thinking about the same idea. I was further along with the proposal than he was, as his idea was just starting to sprout. In a bold move, I called Charles Washington and introduced myself. He was from one of the most prestigious cancer centers in the world, located in Houston, Texas. The M.D. Anderson Cancer Center was very involved in groundbreaking research and innovative methods for treating cancer. And here I was in my eyes, this little guy from Maine—an unknown. At the time, I don't think our entire population in Maine was over a million. We generally relied on the innovative research from Mass General Hospital and other Boston hospitals like the Dana-Farber Cancer Institute. Charles and I talked on the phone multiple times. As an up and coming young leader in our profession, he had a clear-cut vision on how to shape the transitioning field of radiation therapy. It needed to start with a comprehensive textbook written by therapists for therapists.

Hesitant to show his cards, I suggested we each provide several references. After talking to others, we might get a better sense of what we were getting into by combining efforts to write a textbook together instead of competing individually with each other. I listened to the Holy Spirit in hopes of moving the project forward, praying for direction and later found out that he was too. God slowly unfolded the plan involving the two of us. We were both willing to become vulnerable, to gamble and dare greatly. We were all in.

After we agreed to combine efforts—a big black guy from Houston and a little white guy from Maine—we submitted proposals to two publishers, one in Baltimore and one in St. Louis. Within several weeks, we were surprised to receive two contracts, both fairly similar, related to editorial assistance, illustrations, and royalties.

We debated which publisher could better help the project move forward. I proposed to Charles that he be listed as the first author if we accepted the contract from Elsevier Publishing in St. Louis. They offered a ten-thousand-dollar advance to us help defray the costs associated with permissions, artwork, and other publishing expenses. In addition, I had been working with a developmental editor at Elsevier (then Mosby Publishing) for a while and had a good vibe about her commitment to move our project to print. How could we go wrong—her name was Jeanne!

The book was originally published as a three-volume series, building on the content the student would study as they progressed toward their degree. In the second edition, eight years later, we combined the three volumes into one larger textbook with a purple cover. From that point on, students began to refer to the textbook as the "purple book." It took on a life of its own, making it onto shelves throughout our community and even overseas. Charles enjoyed being the ambassador for the book, serving on endless national committees, promoting the book everywhere he traveled and speaking at numerous radiation therapy conferences, even one in Australia. He was good at it.

Before I retired and after contributing to four editions of the book, Charles and I agreed to search for another author/editor to replace me. Megan and I worked closely together through the fifth edition. The plan was for me to mentor her through the process and enhance her editing skills for future editions. She was a pleasure to work with, needed little mentoring, and paid great attention to detail. That skill is essential in writing any book. The fifth edition, my last contribution to the field of radiation therapy, contained a tribute, recognizing all of God's grace poured into this project over the years:

> "With this edition, we are pleased to introduce our third editor, Dr. Megan Trad, who is an associate professor at Texas State University. We would also like to acknowledge and thank Dennis Leaver, one of the founding editors of the textbook, for his efforts in shaping radiation therapy education over the last twenty-five years. His pioneering spirit has helped the educational field of radiation therapy transition from resources originally written by physicists and physicians toward a focused effort of more than five-thousand-two-hundred printed pages and over fifty thousand copies distributed world wide. A majority of that work was contributed by radiation therapists. His impact on the profession is undeniable."[3]

My two colleagues continue to work together on a sixth edition due out soon. It is amazing what God can do with our small gifts—just a few loaves and fishes. The *"Washington and Leaver's Principles and Practice of Radiation Therapy"* textbook has touched countless lives and continues to do so. I believe it remains the most popular comprehensive radiation therapy textbook in the United States and Canada and is widely used to educate radiation therapists in universities, colleges and hospitals. Several years ago, international sales (which include Canada) surpassed domestic sales of the book and included countries such as, England, Ireland, Denmark, Australia, New Zealand, South Africa, Kenya, Uganda, and Singapore. Most recently, the textbook was translated into

---

3. Washington and Leaver, *Principles and Practice of Radiation Therapy*, xiii.

Mandarin in an effort to help educate the growing number of Chinese radiation therapists. The loaves keep multiplying.

For several years after retirement, I enjoyed teaching anatomy and physiology part time at the community college until COVID hit us all so painfully. It became clear to me, even with the call to teach and serve, that delivering the entire course, including a lab on-line did not sit well with me. I shifted gears to volunteering more.

A unique opportunity to travel to Africa with Rotary International and a non-profit group called Partners for World Health attracted me. The mission was to provide training and education to the medical community in the capital city of Kampala. There are a limited number of cancer facilities in Uganda, and they need more modern equipment and training. This trip to Africa helped me to appreciate the need of so many others battling cancer and other diseases. While malaria, tuberculosis and HIV/AIDS are the leading causes of death in the area, treating cancer effectively remains a challenge.

I was impressed with the mission of Partners for World Health and how they made a difference collecting medical supplies and equipment that would otherwise end up in the landfill. After sorting through the discarded medical supplies, evaluating hospital beds and other equipment—what is salvageable is put into a large shipping container and sent by sea or air to places like Africa, Syria or Haiti. I wanted to get more involved and understand how a group of dedicated volunteers accomplished this amazing task.

17

Medical Supplies and Miracles
2016

It was late on a sunny Saturday afternoon when I first met Elizabeth McLellan, the founder of Partners for World Health. I walked into the warehouse in South Portland without an appointment and was greeted by rows of organized shelves filled with discarded medical supplies. Directly in front of me, a towering mound of plastic bags bursting with unsorted medical supplies—surgical instruments, glucose monitors, syringes, and ostomy equipment—caught my eye. The heap, surrounded by hundreds of boxes of various shapes, occupied a good portion of the warehouse, which was about the size of two basketball courts.

Elizabeth emerged from one of the long aisles containing sorted and organized medical supplies. She and I would work closely together in the years to come, both in New England and abroad. I was the only visitor that afternoon, dropping off x-ray equipment from my wife's dental office and radiation therapy-imaging related supplies from the community college, which were all destined for the landfill.

"Is this something you could use?" I asked, gesturing to the donations now organized on a flat pallet. She examined the equipment briefly before nodding. "I'll have Jim, our biomedical engineer, look over the equipment. Everything is tested and thoroughly inspected before we send it out in a container."

We started chatting about my background and how I had obtained the equipment and other medical supplies. As we talked, Elizabeth grabbed one of the plastic bags from the larger pile and dumped it out on a sorting table that had small raised edges added by someone, to keep the stuff from falling off. She was smartly dressed with her hair tied up and had a look of determination and purpose. "This is typical of every hospital we partner with," she said. I recognized some of the items now spilling out on the "macro-sorting" table: boxes of unopened sterile needles, suture kits, rolls of tape, small boxes of alcohol swabs, and gauze pads. Elizabeth caught my eye. "All of this would have ended up in the landfill, Dennis. Thrown away."

"Where do you get all this stuff?" I inquired, as I moved closer to the pile. She explained patiently as she had likely done countless times before, "Donations are picked up by truck or van from hospitals throughout Maine and neighboring states. Right now, we're the only non-profit facility in New England collecting these types of supplies. Oftentimes donations from the hospital may be outdated or discarded unused/unopened after a surgical procedure or just discarded for some other reason. Equipment, such as beds, cardiac monitors, or ultrasound machines are oftentimes upgraded and we get the older model—perfectly usable. Jim checks all that stuff out thoroughly. We also receive supplies and equipment from family members whose loved one has passed."

After the short tour, our conversation drifted to medical waste and the cost of healthcare. I became increasingly interested in this spontaneous tour and wondered how I could become more involved with the many volunteers who kept this operation running smoothly. "If you want to become more involved, fill out an application and sign up for a volunteer orientation session. There's plenty to do," Elizabeth explained, "from driving trucks to sorting all this stuff. We also do medical missions trips to Africa, India, and other places several times a year." I did just that—filled out an application on the spot.

Several months later, I found myself back at the warehouse, nervously sitting in a conference room around a large oval table. Elizabeth, small in stature, projecting a commanding presence was there, along with Dr. Horowitz, a medical oncologist from southern Maine, Nurse Peggy, an oncology nurse navigator also from southern Maine, and Carolyn Johnson, the coordinator of the Maine Chapter of Rotary International. Partners of World Health, in partnership with Rotary International, were planning a medical mission trip to Uganda later that year and were looking for specialized volunteers to join the team. My interview, a mix of questions and discussion, lasted well over an hour.

Carolyn started the meeting. "Dennis, we've reviewed your application. Your experience in radiation therapy is just what we are looking for. I see you have taught for many years at the community college and written several textbooks." Dr. Horowitz leaned in. "We need someone with a background like yours. We've been unable to find a radiation oncology physician to round out our medical team, and your teaching experience would be helpful on the trip." Nurse Peggy nodded. "Teaching doctors, nurses, and other healthcare workers is a big part of the Rotary grant. We'll also be outfitting a new medical oncology wing at St. Francis Hospital in Kampala with equipment and supplies from Partners, but we also need to train their staff." Elizabeth added, "We'll also be working with students at the hospital who are involved in midwifery, nursing, and the medical laboratory programs as well. How would you feel about doing that?"

As the meeting continued, I felt a growing sense of excitement and purpose. These people were motivated in making a difference. This mission was about more than just providing medical care—it was about sharing knowledge and building capacity in a community that desperately needed it. Would I be part of this journey to Africa?

After leaving the room while they discussed my responses to the questions, my references, and other information provided in the application, I wandered around and inspected shelf after shelf of medical supplies, meticulously sorted and labeled, stacked on row after row of old metal shelving. It was like a food bank, but instead of food stacked on the shelves, there were medical supplies.

Over the next few months, I worked closely with Elizabeth, Carolyn from Rotary International, and Dr. Horowitz to organize the power-point presentations needed for the teaching sessions and prepare other equipment for the mission. Three additional oncology nurses planned to join the team. Their specialty involved chemotherapy and palliative care. Interestingly, the thirty-five percent survival rate in Uganda at the time was similar to that found in the United States when I first began working in radiation therapy in the late 1970's.

Finally, the day came to depart for Uganda from Logan airport. The journey included a stopover in Amsterdam and Rwanda before our plane descended over the lush landscape surrounding Lake Victoria and into Entebbe airport. I felt a mix of nervousness, excitement, and fatigue.

The heat and humidity hit us immediately. The air was thick, buzzing with the familiar sounds of airport traffic. We were greeted by several representatives from the rotary clubs and a doctor from St. Francis Hospital, who helped us load supplies into a waiting van. The drive to the hospital took us through more traffic and the vibrant bustling streets of a busy city, a stark contrast to the calm roads of Maine.

Moving through the crowded streets of Kampala is an experience that engages all the senses. The city is humming with constant activity: car horns blaring, motorcycles weaving in and out of traffic, and vendors calling out from crowded market stalls. Boda-bodas, a type of motor scooter taxi constantly zips past pedestrians, cars and buses, sometimes using part of the sidewalk to get around traffic. The dusty, dry air is filled with the rich aromas of street food, from grilled meats to fried plantains.

In the paved streets of the downtown area, people flow like a river through the narrow alleyways and roads, each with a purpose, whether it's heading to work, shopping, or simply going about their daily routines. There are very few street lights. Children in their school uniform are seen early in the morning and again late in the day. Most children are enrolled in private school and are dressed in a distinctive colorful uniform that proudly represents their school. Despite the chaos, there's a sense of purpose in the way people interact; making the journey through Kampala each day not just a trip, but a glimpse into the heartbeat of Uganda. Each of us were staying with a host family, making the commute into and out of the city each day a lengthy stimulating adventure.

At the hospital, we were welcomed warmly by the staff. Dr. Mutesi, the head of the new oncology wing, shook everyone's hand firmly and looked us in the eye. "Welcome. Welcome to each of you. We've been eagerly waiting the team's arrival. Your loving support is so valuable to us. Thank you, thank you for coming."

When we toured the nearly empty two story twenty-four-bed hospital, built by the Greater Kampala Rotarians two years earlier, I was struck by the resourcefulness and dedication of the staff. Despite limited resources, their commitment to patient care was evident. The new oncology wing, surrounded by a beautiful grassy area and small gardens, was a work in progress, but the potential was clear. The rooms were filled with sunlight, and the smell of fresh paint mingled with the aroma of the city. Waving in the wind on clothes lines in a field near the oncology wing were that day's laundry—an example of resourcefulness. Cancer patients were seen, examined, and treated on an outpatient basis, as there were no beds yet.

Sixteen refurbished modern Stryker hospital beds on one of the containers, we learned later, would arrive after our departure, due to delays at the border crossing into Kenya. The valuable equipment and medical supplies, packed by volunteers at Partners for World Health, would need to wait. We had plenty to do with the supplies we carried into Entebbe. Each of us was responsible for a donated L.L. Bean duffle bag on wheels, filled with forty-nine and one-half pounds of valuable medical supplies—a second checked bag, x-rayed and inspected at the airport.

Our early days were filled with unpacking and organizing the supplies, and the training scheduled each morning—three separate sessions, leaving time for questions and discussion. Dr. Horowitz saw chemotherapy patients each day. Most of us spent numerous hours with the local doctors, medical students, and nurses; demonstrating techniques and sharing knowledge specific to cancer prevention, diagnosis and treatment. I even assisted once on a long shift in the emergency room with one of our doctors, mostly fetching needed medical supplies.

Additionally, the nursing and midwifery students were especially eager to learn—their enthusiasm was infectious. They were located in a large building surrounded by several over crowded dorms in an area separate from the walled hospital compound. For many of the students this was there first chance to gain a lifelong skill.

The weeks passed and the bond between our team, the hospital staff, and local Rotary Clubs grew stronger. We faced challenges, from power outages, intense traffic each day, early morning roosters, and unexpected delays, but we learned and worked together.

I especially bonded with Sr. Garetti, a breast cancer surgeon at St. Francis Hospital. A bit overweight with small tufts of white hair peeking out from under her nun's habit, she moved with a slight limp that did little to hinder her determined stride. Her presence projected a quiet strength, a testament of her commitment to helping the poor. She had an uncanny ability to bring light into the lives of her cancer patients. She often joked that her laughter was a secret ingredient in their treatment plan, a medicine as potent as any drug. Her quick quips and playful banter about God made the frightening hospital environment feel warmer, more human. "I may not have a cure for cancer," she'd say with her dark brown eyes, "but I can definitely cure a bad mood." Her humor was a bridge, connecting her deeply with those she cared for, and turning moments of fear into shared smiles. I will always remember her style and how she shared God's love with all her heart.

In preparing to leave Uganda, I sensed this was just the beginning. Two years later, I would return a second time with Jeanne. The connections we made with locals, hospital staff and Rotary

International members and the knowledge we shared would continue to grow, building a foundation for better healthcare in the region. And for me, it was a reminder of the power of collaboration and compassion.

It wasn't long after returning to Maine that I became more involved with Partners for World Health: spreading the word, loading containers, and picking up supplies. After tagging along with one of the warehouse managers, I was drawn into interacting with people in the community and personnel at the hospitals during our pick-ups, usually in a large box truck, complete with a hydraulic lift-gate for the really heavy stuff. Many of the hospitals were familiar to me from my days of visiting radiation therapy students where they were assigned to a clinical rotation.

Learning to effectively use the pallet jack increased with time. Moving stuff around the warehouse was relatively easy compared to loading or unloading a pallet onto the lift-gate. Jeremy gently reminded me, "Dennis, if something begins to fall off the truck or lift-gate, let it go." I responded, "Yeah, it's all donated stuff, destined for the landfill until we came along." Jeremy laughed and said, "The important thing to remember is to keep it safe and not get hurt." I smiled at him, asking, "Have you ever dropped anything?" He nodded and said, "Just once. Right here in the parking lot, trying to get a pallet of PPE (personal protective equipment) off the truck and into one of our rented storage containers out back. We use those for overflow. The entire pallet fell off the lift-gate and crashed to the ground. This was during COVID, and the pallet had boxes of N95 masks and gowns. No harm done. We reassembled the boxes on the pallet."

A typical volunteer shift involved driving the truck throughout Maine and New Hampshire, or sometimes Boston. We were eager to load whatever they had for us, which would otherwise be discarded. Most shifts, we would return to one of the warehouses with a load of medical supplies shrink-wrapped on six to eight pallets. Anything considered "medical supplies" was usually donated in a cardboard box or heavy-duty clear plastic bag, unloaded, weighed and logged in. It would then be sorted by other volunteers with expertise in recognizing and evaluating things like surgical, respiratory, or cardiovascular supplies. Most everything was usable. All biomedical equipment arrived at our Portland warehouse for evaluation and testing. At one point, we shared this warehouse with a printing company, making it a challenge when both groups required extra space to store or inspect their merchandise.

Wheelchairs, hospital beds, and stretchers arrived at a separate warehouse, also in Portland. Equipment such as walkers, crutches, shower stools, and potty chairs, all categorized as DME or durable medical equipment, made its way to a section in the warehouse where it would be evaluated, tested, and/or repaired. We also had another name for DME, as it was difficult to stack and organize. It required a lot of valuable space.

We would usually make monthly trips to the metal recycling facility nearby, keeping some of this unrepairable stuff out of the landfill. Last year we filled and shipped more than twenty containers around the world. Standard shipping containers are typically forty feet long, eight feet wide, and about eight and one-half feet tall. Each container is packed with about three-hundred-fifty thousand dollars' worth of refurbished medical equipment and supplies, partially selected by the receiving country. For example, when we send supplies to Ukraine, they prefer surgical equipment, suture material, bandages, and other medical supplies for war related injuries. A recent container to Tanzania contained over thirty-six hospital beds used to fill a new hospital wing in the capital city of Dodoma.

Every container we ship is packed by volunteers. The shipment is carefully evaluated by a special volunteer team that calculates maximize volume and weight restrictions to meet customs criteria in the receiving country. A group of effective volunteers can usually pack a container in three to four hours and are generally very good at the old puzzle game called Tetris. The game where you quickly organize various shaped falling blocks snuggly against one another. Elizabeth, our founder, is always telling people, "we don't ship air."

Medical Supplies and Miracles

Working with Partners for World Health has felt like participating in a modern-day miracle. It's very similar to Jesus multiplying the loaves and fishes. Just as Jesus took a small offering and transformed it into a feast that fed thousands, we at Partners for World Health take donated medical supplies—and through our collective efforts, turn them into life-saving resources for communities around the world, affecting thousands. Each box of equipment, every pallet of supplies is multiplied in impact, reaching far beyond what we could have imagined, providing hope and healing to those in need. Our work is a testament to the power of ingenuity, generosity and teamwork—transforming small contributions from the community into containers of compassion. We hear countless testimonies of how people feel loved by the donations, such as this one from Ukraine:

> "This week, we performed a massive delivery of medical supplies to the Chornomorsk hospital in the Odessa region of south Ukraine. It will improve the lives of patients and the hospital's ability to offer medical care to the many civilians affected by the war. It took us and our great partners, Operation SafeDrop, three trips in our trucks to deliver all the hospital beds, wheelchairs and a broad range of medical supplies—over one hundred thirty items from orthopedic to surgical supplies, syringes, gloves, and disinfectants. We are deeply thankful to our partners who played a crucial role at various stages of the delivery. Your support has made a significant difference in the lives of the patients at Chornomorsk hospital. Those who participated included; Partners for World Health, Tullman Community Ventures, Oleksandr Roytburg and Operation SafeDrop Logistics Cluster. Thank you so much!"[1]

---

1. Partners for World Health, "UAid Direct is with UAid Direct USA," paras. 1.

18

Wilderness to Grace

2025

LOOKING IN THE REARVIEW mirror, I can now see more clearly the path I have traveled since leaving the lush marijuana growing fields of Humboldt County. The "Ragged Road" has presented its share of twists and turns, yet it has been rich with meaningful challenges, eye-opening lessons, and a profound sense of purpose. I recognize now that my journey has been guided by an invisible hand—one I have come to understand as God's. This journey has not merely been about seeking direction in life but also about cultivating the faith to trust that direction. Despite the inevitability of falling, it was crucial for me not to remain fallen, but to get up again. We all stumble and make mistakes; falling is a part of life, but I didn't want it to define me.

There was a time when I sought validation from those around me—through getting things done, or recognition from others, and even through experiences that I thought would make me whole. However, amidst some of the challenges I faced, I realized these external pursuits were distractions from the true journey that unfolds within. It was during these solitary moments—whether traveling from California, exploring the Allagash, or witnessing the birth of my son—that I began to grasp the profound depth of God's love and the peace that comes from surrendering to it. I once humbly attached a light blue bumper sticker on my pickup truck after moving to Maine that proclaimed, "Let Go and Let God." This served as a valuable reminder in those early days, and it remains a thought I revisit from time to time.

Love, too, has been a central part of this journey—not just the love of family and friends, but a deeper, more encompassing love that transcends what we can see. I have learned that love manifests in the smallest of moments: in helping a friend, in teaching a student, or in the way we listen to one another. It is also reflected in how we treat ourselves after we fall, learning to "let go" and embrace the future. Forgiveness has been essential to that part of my journey, as Jesus teaches that God will not forgive us if we do not forgive others.

As I sit here today, I realize that the road I've been traveling is not as ragged as it used to be, not because life has become easier or more predictable, but because my perspective has changed. The road ahead still remains uncertain, yet I now walk it guided by faith and love. What once felt like a series of random events has become a purposeful journey, with each challenge and setback contributing to my understanding and awareness.

Partway through my journey on the "Ragged Road," I realized that my primary gift was teaching. Your gift may differ, but I believe we all possess unique gifts according to the grace bestowed upon us. We can sometimes utilize these gifts to uplift and encourage others. I am continually amazed at how God can take our small offerings and multiply its impact, creating powerful ripple effects.

Reaching out and seeking a relationship with God often guides us toward meaningful experiences. This spiritual connection invites us to reflect on our purpose and gifts. Are we open to recognizing the signs of this relationship in our daily lives? How does our understanding of spirituality influence our interactions with others?

Learning is an essential part of this journey, shaping our growth and understanding of our purpose. It is through learning that we discover what it means to be in a place that matters—whether that's a physical place, a community, or in a relationship. How do we choose or guide the circumstances that help contribute to our sense of purpose? What lessons do these places teach us about ourselves and our connections with our friends, family, and community?

Having true friends who support us and encourage us is essential in traveling along our sometimes ragged road. These relationships deepen our lives and help us to cultivate an understanding of both ourselves and the world. How do our friendships reflect our spiritual journey? In what ways do they encourage us to continue learning and growing?

Ultimately, the journey is not just about reaching a destination. It is about the growth that occurs along the way, and the faith that is tested and developed. I've come to realize that life's most important journey is the one we take inwardly. And while the road may still be ragged at times, it is nice to know we need not walk it alone.

Bibliography

Almasri, Eyad, and Firas Alawneh. "Petra—Holy City from the Perspective of Art, Architecture, Inscriptions and Other Features." Studies in Ancient Art and Civilization 22 (June 2018), accessed May 23, 2023. https://doi.org/10.12797/SAAC.22.2018.22.04.

Beecham, Jack. "CAMP Final Report 1988," accessed January 5, 2023. https://specialcollections.humboldt.edu/sites/default/files/camp1988.pdf.

Bellini, Peter. "Do You Renounce Satan? A Glance at the Christian Baptismal Vows of Renunciation." Firebrand, accessed August 13, 2024. https://firebrandmag.com/articles/do-you-renounce-satan-a-glance-at-the-christian-baptismal-vows-of-renunciation.

Biblical Archaeology Society Staff. "The House of Peter: The Home of Jesus in Capernaum? How the Remnants of the Humble Dwelling of Jesus in Capernaum Illuminate How Christianity Began," accessed December 18, 2023. https://www.biblicalarchaeology.org/daily/biblical-sites-places/biblical-archaeology-sites/the-house-of-peter-the-home-of-jesus-in-capernaum/.

Bird, Chad. *Night Driving: Notes From a Prodigal Soul.* Grand Rapids: Wm. B. Eerdmans, 2017.

Brand, Paul, and Philip Yancey. *Fearfully and Wonderfully Made.* Grand Rapids: Zondervan, 1980.

Brown, Brené. Host, Dare to Lead Podcast, "Brené with Dr. Maya Shanker on Courage in the Midst of Change." Brené Brown, LLC, November 8, 2021, accessed January 31, 2024. https://brenebrown.com/podcast/courage-in-the-midst-of-change/.

Jethani, Skye. *With.* Nashville: Thomas Nelson, 2011.

Karr, Mary. *The Art of Memoir.* New York: Harper Perennial, 2016.

Lindsay, Leon. "California Narc Agents Attack Marijuana at its Roots." *Christian Science Monitor,* October 22, 1982, 12:10 p.m. ET. https://www.csmonitor.com/1982/1022/102261.html

BIBLIOGRAPHY

Martignetti, Rick. *Hidden Beauty: Reflections on Saint Bonaventure's Tree of Life*. Indianapolis: Tau, 2013.

———. *Perfect Love*. Indianapolis: Tau, 2022.

Mendel, William. "Counterdrug Strategy—Elusive Victory: From Blast Furnace to Green Sweep," accessed May 25, 2023. https://web.archive.org/web/20170513054206/http:/fmso.leavenworth.army.mil/documents/ilusive.htm.

Milstein, Mati. "Petra." *National Geographic*, Accessed May 23, 2023. https://www.nationalgeographic.com/history/article/lost-city-petra.

Merton, Thomas. *He Is Risen*. Boston: Argus Communications, Ex-Monastery Library Edition, 1975.

———. *Seven Story Mountain*. New York: Harcourt-Brace, 1978.

Nouwen, Henri. *The Return of the Prodigal Son*. New York: Doubleday, 1992.

Partners for World Health (@partnersforworldhealth). "UAid Direct is with UAid Direct USA." Facebook, September 18, 2024. https://www.facebook.com/PartnersForWorldHealth/posts/pfbidoMfnrUuszhQzox6Nhg2Yv514ebVNiNgaR9NbLbrp4dLCVqjKPio4eKWHz4rLrgGVYl.

Rohr, Richard. "Embracing the Fire of Transformation." The Center for Action and Contemplation (blog). Jul-Sep 2024. https://cac.org/daily-meditations/2024-daily-meditations-theme-radical-resilience/.

———. *Everything Belongs: the Gift of Contemplative Prayer*. New York: The Crossroads, 2003.

———. *Immortal Diamond*. Hoboken: John Wiley & Sons, Inc., 2013.

Scott, S. *Fierce Conversations: Achieving Success at Work and in Life One Conversation at a Time*. Viking, 2002.

Schmidt, William. "Millions in South Treated to a Rare View of Solar Eclipse," *New York Times*, May 31, 1984, 3:00 p.m. EST. https://www.nytimes.com/1984/05/31/us/millions-in-south-treated-to-rare-view-of-solar-eclipse.html.

Washington, C.M., and Dennis Leaver. *Washington and Leaver's Principles and Practice of Radiation Therapy*. 5th ed. St. Louis: Elsevier, 2021.

Wright, Vinita Hampton. *The Art of Spiritual Writing*. Chicago: Loyola, 2013.

Zugibe, Frederick T. *The Crucifixion of Jesus, Completely Revised and Expanded: A Forensic Inquiry*. M. Evans and Company, Inc., New York, 2005.

www.ingramcontent.com/pod-product-compliance
Lightning Source LLC
Chambersburg PA
CBHW071724090426
42738CB00009B/1869